Contents

Diabetes Mellitus, Volume XII, Number 3, July 2013
After reading *Diabetes Mellitus*, go to:
www.clinicalupdates.org

- Complete and submit the CME questions online—automatically add 5 CME credits to your College cognate transcript. CME credit is available for all titles posted online.
- View links to resources related to diabetes mellitus.
  - American College of Obstetricians and Gynecologists
    www.acog.org
  - American Diabetes Association
    www.diabetes.org
  - American Geriatrics Society
    www.americangeriatrics.org
  - Centers for Disease Control and Prevention
    www.cdc.gov
  - Institute of Medicine
    www.iom.edu
  - National Center for Complementary and Alternative Medicine
    nccam.nih.gov
  - National Institute of Diabetes and Digestive and Kidney Diseases
    www2.niddk.nih.gov
  - U.S. Department of Health and Human Services
    www.hhs.gov
- Order College patient education material.
- See full text of past issues and any relevant changes or updates.

VOLUME XII, NUMBER 3, JULY 2013

CLINICAL UPDATES IN WOMEN'S HEALTH CARE

Diabetes Mellitus

Donald R. Coustan, MD
Department of Obstetrics and Gynecology
Warren Alpert Medical School of Brown University
Division of Maternal–Fetal Medicine
Women and Infants Hospital of Rhode Island
Providence, Rhode Island

The American College of
Obstetricians and Gynecologists
WOMEN'S HEALTH CARE PHYSICIANS

Clinical Updates in Women's Health Care is published quarterly by the American College of Obstetricians and Gynecologists (the College). This series represents the knowledge and experience of the authors and does not necessarily reflect the policy of the American College of Obstetricians and Gynecologists. The recommendations do not dictate an exclusive course of treatment or of practice. Variations taking into account the needs of the individual patient, resources, and limitations unique to the institution or type of practice may be appropriate.

ISSN: 1536-3619
ISBN: 978-1-934984-23-9

12345/76543   CU056

Continuing Medical Education

Objectives

This monograph is designed to enable obstetrician–gynecologists to do the following:

- Understand the pathophysiology and clinical approaches for the management of type 1 diabetes mellitus and the prevention and management of type 2 diabetes mellitus and their acute and chronic complications
- Identify risk factors for diabetes mellitus and screen patients accordingly
- Apply testing techniques and criteria for the diagnosis of diabetes mellitus
- Counsel patients regarding the prevention and management of diabetes mellitus
- Understand the effect of maternal diabetes mellitus on intrauterine development, the effect of pregnancy on intermediary metabolism, and clinical approaches to the management of diabetes mellitus during pregnancy
- Develop a team approach to the treatment of type 1 diabetes mellitus and type 2 diabetes mellitus

ACCME Accreditation

The American College of Obstetricians and Gynecologists is accredited by the Accreditation Council for Continuing Medical Education (ACCME) to provide continuing medical education for physicians.

AMA PRA Category 1 Credit™

The American College of Obstetricians and Gynecologists designates this enduring activity for a maximum of 5 AMA PRA Category 1 Credit(s)™. Physicians should only claim credit commensurate with the extent of their participation in the activity.

College Cognate Credit

The American College of Obstetricians and Gynecologists designates this enduring activity for a maximum of 5 Category 1 College Cognate Credits. The College has a reciprocity agreement with the AMA that allows AMA PRA Category 1 Credit(s)™ to be equivalent to College Cognate Credits.

Credit for *Clinical Updates in Women's Health Care: Diabetes Mellitus*, Volume XII, Number 3, July 2013, is initially available through December 2016. During that year, the unit will be re-evaluated. If the content remains current, credit is extended for an additional 3 years.

Disclosure Statement

Current guidelines state that continuing medical education (CME) providers must ensure that CME activities are free from the control of any commercial interest. All authors, editorial board members, and reviewers declare that neither they nor any business associate nor any member of their immediate families has material interest, financial interest, or other relationships with any company manufacturing commercial products relative to the topics included in this publication or with any provider of commercial services discussed in this publication except for Morton Stenchever, MD, who has financial interests in Merck, Pfizer, Bristol Myers, GlaxoSmithKline, and Amgen; Raul Artal, MD, who has been involved with clinical trials with Nascent, Solvay, Xenodyne, Symbollon Pharmaceuticals, and Columbia Laboratories; and Julia Schlam Edelman, MD, who has financial interests in Alnylam Pharmaceuticals and Intelligent Bio-Systems. Any conflicts have been resolved through group and outside review of all content.

See page iv for submission of CME credits.

Foreword

We are clearly experiencing an epidemic of diabetes mellitus, which undoubtedly relates directly to the increase in prevalence of overweight and obese individuals. As a result of this trend, obstetrician–gynecologists are providing care for increasing numbers of women of all ages with diabetes, thus encountering problems, such as gestational diabetes mellitus, women's general health issues, and increased health risks for women with diabetes mellitus. Therefore, it is important for the obstetrician–gynecologist to be well versed in the latest diagnostic and therapeutic measures necessary to provide appropriate care for and provide referrals to specialists for patients who are at high risk of morbidity and mortality resulting from diabetes mellitus. We have previously published two monographs on diabetes, but the increasing prevalence of diabetes that occurs in our patients and the advances in care that have taken place have prompted this newest publication. It is prepared by a well-known diabetes specialist and should bring our readers up to the current state of diabetes management. Diabetes mellitus is having a major effect on the practice of obstetrics and gynecology and requires knowledge of the latest information to help us provide proper care for our patients affected by this condition.

Morton A. Stenchever, MD
Editor

ABSTRACT: *Diabetes mellitus has reached epidemic proportions in the United States; more than one third of all adult Americans have either diabetes mellitus or prediabetes (characterized by impaired fasting glucose, impaired glucose tolerance, or both) (1). In large part due to the epidemic of obesity, type 2 diabetes mellitus is now appearing at younger ages. Women's health care providers encounter increasing numbers of women who have diabetes mellitus during their reproductive years, during pregnancy, and in the course of gynecologic care. Up-to-date information regarding the risk factors for diabetes mellitus, its early detection, possible prevention, and management will allow physicians to develop strategies to improve the quality of their patients' lives and ameliorate the long-term effects of diabetes mellitus.*

At the time of the previous edition of this monograph in 2007, 9.3% of Americans older than 19 years had diabetes (2). Currently, according to the most recent National Health and Nutrition Examination Survey (NHANES) report, between 2005 and 2008, the prevalence of diabetes increased by 21%, and now 11.3% of adult Americans have diabetes, including 10.8% of women and 11.8% of men (1). One fourth of these individuals are unaware of their condition. An additional 35% of adult Americans have prediabetes. The prevalence of diabetes is clearly on the rise in the United States, as it is around the world. It is a chilling thought that almost one half of adult Americans now have diabetes or prediabetes.

Diabetes is more common among Hispanic individuals and in non-Hispanic blacks than in non-Hispanic whites and Asian Americans, but it is increasing in all of these groups. Diabetes increases with age; 50% of Americans aged 65 years and older have prediabetes, and 26.9% of Americans aged 65 years and older have diabetes (1). Diabetes mellitus is a serious disease; untreated it can lead to a host of complications, including blindness, kidney

1

failure, heart attacks, strokes, and amputations. Diabetes mellitus was the seventh leading recorded cause of death in the United States in 2007, and this represents underreporting (1). Studies have found that only 35–40% of death certificates of individuals with diabetes mellitus have that diagnosis listed anywhere on the form. Individuals with diabetes mellitus are twice as likely to die in a given year as those of a similar age without diabetes (1).

A number of diabetic problems are unique to women. Preexisting diabetes mellitus can have devastating effects on pregnancy, including birth defects, prematurity, macrosomia, and stillbirth. Gestational diabetes mellitus (GDM), which appears during pregnancy and most often disappears after delivery, can cause fetal macrosomia and stillbirth and is highly predictive of subsequent diabetes mellitus in the mother. The offspring of women with preexisting diabetes mellitus and, to some extent, GDM are prone to neonatal hypoglycemia, plethora, hyperbilirubinemia, and a number of other problems. Also, they are prone to childhood obesity and diabetes mellitus.

Many of the complications of diabetes mellitus can be reduced or prevented by identifying patients who are at risk of the disease and implementing prevention strategies, early diagnosis, and intensive management that involves the patient and the health care team. Obstetrician–gynecologists can contribute greatly to this effort. Because so many women regard their obstetrician–gynecologists as their primary care providers, the opportunity exists to evaluate risk factors, counsel patients regarding the prevention of diabetes mellitus, establish early diagnoses, and participate in long-term care of women at risk of diabetes mellitus or those who have the disease. In addition, reproductive care specialists who provide care for pregnant women have the opportunity to diagnose preexisting diabetes mellitus during early pregnancy, test for GDM as pregnancy progresses, and provide the necessary management for pregnant women affected by these conditions.

Types of Diabetes Mellitus

All types of diabetes mellitus are characterized by chronic hyperglycemia. When the pancreas produces too little insulin or no insulin at all or when insulin is not effective in regulating the level of sugar in the blood because of insulin resistance in liver, muscle, or adipose tissue, hyperglycemia results. Currently, the classification of diabetes mellitus is based on presumed etiology and includes four types (3):

1. Type 1 diabetes mellitus is attributed to complete failure of the pancreatic β-cells to secrete insulin, resulting in absolute insulin deficiency. Type 1 diabetes mellitus was formerly called "juvenile diabetes" because typically it occurred in people younger than 30 years. However, type 1 diabetes mellitus can manifest at older ages, and not all children or young adults with diabetes mellitus have type 1 disease, so this nomenclature was abandoned. Type 1 diabetes mellitus also was once called "insulin-dependent diabetes." This label was intended to emphasize the fact that individuals with this type of diabetes required exogenous insulin to avoid diabetic ketoacidosis. However, much confusion arose between "insulin-dependent" and "insulin-treated" nomenclatures. Individuals with type 2 diabetes mellitus frequently are treated with insulin although they are not prone to experience ketosis and, thus, are not truly dependent on insulin.

2. Type 2 diabetes mellitus is attributed to a combination of relative insulin secretory deficiency, which generally is progressive, and insulin resistance in various organs, such as liver, muscle, and adipose tissue. Type 2 diabetes mellitus was once called "adult-onset diabetes," but this nomenclature was abandoned because of the increasingly frequent appearance of this type of diabetes in younger individuals and because some individuals whose diabetes is first apparent after the age of 30 years have type 1 diabetes. It also was once called "non–insulin-dependent diabetes" but, as noted earlier, some individuals with type 2 diabetes mellitus are treated with insulin, which results in confusion over the former nomenclature.

3. Diabetes mellitus is a condition related to causes other than those outlined previously, such as genetic forms of inadequate insulin action or secretion; pancreatic diseases, such as cystic fibrosis or traumatic or surgical pancreatectomy;

or drug-induced diabetes, such as that seen with certain medications used to treat human immunodeficiency virus (HIV).

4. Gestational diabetes mellitus is diabetes mellitus with onset or first recognition during pregnancy.

 Basic Science Update

Mechanisms of Disease

An understanding of the mechanisms of disease is critical to comprehending the reasons behind various diagnostic and therapeutic approaches. In this section, the mechanisms of disease will be considered as they related to various forms of diabetes. Sufficient details are provided to inform clinical care providers, but many of the molecular details are beyond the scope of this monograph.

TYPE 1 DIABETES MELLITUS

Type 1 diabetes mellitus generally is considered to be caused by autoimmune mechanisms. Most individuals with type 1 diabetes mellitus have detectable markers for autoimmunity, most commonly glutamic acid decarboxylase antibodies, insulin autoantibodies, and islet cell antibodies. Although not all individuals with these antibodies have the disease, a high proportion will develop type 1 diabetes mellitus over time. The development of type 1 diabetes mellitus appears to require an environmental trigger superimposed on genetic factors that render the individual susceptible. Certain histocompatibility antigens are associated with an increased likelihood of type 1 diabetes mellitus. These include specific subtypes of the human leukocyte antigens DR and DQ. Other human leukocyte antigen DR and DQ subtypes appear to be protective against type 1 diabetes mellitus. The mechanisms by which these subtypes enhance or diminish the likelihood of type 1 diabetes mellitus currently are under study. A number of other loci also have been associated with type 1 diabetes mellitus. For example, the *IDDM2* locus includes a noncoding region of the insulin gene that encompasses variable number tandem repeats. Polymorphisms in this region appear to confer an increased risk of diabetes mellitus.

Patients with Wolfram syndrome, an autosomal recessive disorder in which β-cells are absent from the pancreas, demonstrate type 1 diabetes mellitus, diabetes insipidus, optic atrophy, neural deafness, and hypogonadism.

TYPE 2 DIABETES MELLITUS

Type 2 diabetes mellitus is a heterogeneous group of conditions that share common features, including insulin resistance (decreased insulin action) and relatively reduced β-cell function. Although both features appear to be necessary for the development of type 2 diabetes mellitus, it is somewhat controversial as to whether one feature precedes the other and in which order. In some studies, insulin resistance could be detected for many years before the development of type 2 diabetes mellitus, accompanied by increased insulin secretion and then by decreased insulin secretion followed by the appearance of diabetes (4–6). However, it also can be argued that in the face of insulin resistance, insulin secretion should have been even higher, and thus, the secretory defect was present from early on.

Environmental Factors

Genetic and environmental factors modify type 1 diabetes mellitus and type 2 diabetes mellitus. Central obesity, which diminishes insulin sensitivity, is the most significant contributor to the development of type 2 diabetes mellitus in many populations. Adipose tissue releases a number of substances that, either by excess or by deficiency, are likely contributory to insulin resistance. Leptin is secreted by adipocytes and has an inhibitory effect on the hypothalamus to decrease appetite; leptin deficiency and leptin resistance may be associated with obesity and insulin resistance. It is possible that leptin also is a regulator of pancreatic β-cell function, which would provide a link between obesity and diminished insulin secretion. Tumor necrosis factor α is an inflammatory cytokine released from adipose tissue and may reduce insulin

sensitivity. Adiponectin, another cytokine released from adipocytes, may increase insulin sensitivity, and its deficiency (or a
receptor deficiency) may predispose to diabetes. All of these
proposed mechanisms, as well as the potential role of a number
of other cytokines, chemokines, and other proteins, await further
elucidation.

Pancreatic β-cells secrete insulin in response to increased
glucose levels, and glucose entry into these cells is mediated to
some extent by glucose transporter 2, which in animal models
may be diminished by a high-fat diet, which further leads to
impaired insulin secretion.

Genetic Factors

Type 2 diabetes mellitus results from a combination of multiple
genetic and environmental contributors, not a single cause, nor
even a small number of causes. Monozygotic twin studies demonstrate a high level of concordance for type 2 diabetes mellitus
(7). Diabetes and prediabetes are markedly increased among
first-degree relatives of individuals with type 2 diabetes mellitus. A great variation exists in the prevalence of type 2 diabetes
mellitus between members of different ethnic groups who live in
the same environment as well as between members of the same
ethnic group who live in different environments, which suggests
the contributions of genetics and environment to the development of type 2 disease.

Type 2 diabetes mellitus is considered a polygenic disorder.
As molecular medicine has progressed, an ever-increasing number
of genetic associations with type 2 diabetes mellitus have been
discovered. Genome-wide association studies have identified
susceptibility loci in genes coding for pancreatic cell growth and
development, islet cell survival, insulin synthesis, and insulin
release in various populations (8). Although a number of insulin
receptor gene mutations are associated with insulin resistance
syndromes, most forms of type 2 diabetes mellitus are likely
caused by a postreceptor defect. Candidates for this role include
genes that code for glycogen synthase, insulin receptor substrates,
and transcription factors for adipocyte differentiation.

Metabolic Syndrome

Metabolic syndrome, also known as insulin resistance syndrome or syndrome X, is a cluster of characteristic features that are risk factors for diabetes and cardiovascular (CV) disease. Prominent among these are insulin resistance, hyperinsulinemia, prediabetes or type 2 diabetes mellitus, hypertension, dyslipidemia (high triglyceride levels plus or minus low high-density lipoprotein [HDL] cholesterol levels), and coronary artery disease. Many patients with metabolic syndrome are centrally obese and many have polycystic ovary syndrome (PCOS) with acanthosis nigricans. A number of definitions are currently in use; one, which was developed by the National Cholesterol Education Program Adult Treatment Panel III and endorsed by the American Heart Association and the National Heart, Lung, and Blood Institute of the National Institutes of Health (NIH), requires any three of the following five traits to establish the diagnosis (9):

1. Abdominal obesity (waist circumference in women greater than 88 cm [35 in])

2. Serum triglyceride level, 150 mg/dL or more, or drug treatment for elevated triglyceride level

3. Serum HDL cholesterol level, less than 50 mg/dL in women, or drug treatment for low HDL cholesterol level

4. Blood pressure, 130 mm Hg or higher systolic and 85 mm Hg or higher diastolic, or drug treatment for high blood pressure

5. Fasting plasma glucose level, 100 mg/dL or more, or drug treatment for elevated blood glucose level

Other definitions, which differ only slightly from that described previously, also have been proposed and are in use. When data from the NHANES in 2003–2006 were examined, 34% of adults older than 20 years in the United States met the criteria for metabolic syndrome (10). Individuals with metabolic syndrome are at a significantly increased risk of developing diabetes (if it has not already manifested) and coronary artery disease. Metabolic syndrome likely is a major contributor to the epidemic of type 2 diabetes mellitus experienced around the world.

Diabetes Mellitus Related to Other Causes

SINGLE-GENE DISORDERS

At one time, a third type of diabetes was labeled "MODY" ("maturity onset diabetes in the young"); it was characterized by mild type 2 diabetes mellitus that presented in individuals generally younger than 25 years and was strongly transmitted in families as an autosomal dominant condition. Six types of MODY have been described; each has now been associated with a specific molecular disorder (11). The label MODY has been largely abandoned because it is now understood as a heterogeneous group of primarily single-gene defects. Many of these single-gene defects result from any of multiple mutations in the particular gene that lead to phenotypic heterogeneity even within a particular disorder. For example, the most common MODY condition, formerly known as MODY 3, involves the gene for *hepatocyte nuclear factor 1 alpha*, which is located on chromosome 12 and affects liver cells, pancreatic α-cells, pancreatic β-cells, and polypeptide cells of the pancreas. This disorder results in decreased glucose stimulated insulin secretion. Insulin sensitivity apparently is not impaired. Individuals with this mutation have mild elevations in fasting glucose levels, but their postprandial glucose levels tend to increase over time; many patients need oral antidiabetic agents and a significant proportion of patients end up using insulin. Patients with such mutations are susceptible to all the complications seen in type 1 diabetes mellitus and type 2 diabetes mellitus.

The entity formerly called MODY 2 is related to any of a large number of mutations (more than 100 have been described) in the glucokinase gene, which likely functions as a glucose sensor in the pancreatic β-cells. Individuals who are homozygous for glucokinase gene mutations have severe neonatal diabetes, which persists throughout life and requires insulin replacement. Individuals who are heterozygous generally have mild type 2 diabetes mellitus and are treated with diet. Female carriers are likely to develop GDM when they are pregnant, but their infants do not tend to be macrosomic, perhaps because they are likely to inherit the same mutation, which diminishes pancreatic insulin responsiveness to ambient glucose levels.

The other single-gene disorders associated with what was once called MODY are much less common, generally being limited to small numbers of specific families or kinships. Genetic array chips are used to search for the many possible mutations, but their use is primarily a research tool, which is quite expensive now.

MATERNALLY INHERITED DIABETES MELLITUS AND DEAFNESS

Maternally inherited diabetes and deafness is a single-gene mutation, but it differs from those mutations described in the previous section in being transmitted maternally through mitochondrial DNA rather than nuclear DNA. A specific locus on transfer RNA is altered. Individuals with this disorder have progressive diabetes mellitus, usually treatable with oral insulin secretogogues early in its course but progressing to insulin dependence later on. The onset generally is in the fourth decade of life. Because the defect is in insulin secretion rather than insulin sensitivity, metformin typically is not useful and may cause lactic acidosis. Affected individuals also have sensorineural hearing loss.

PANCREATIC DISEASES

Conditions that adversely affect the exocrine pancreas also may lead to diabetes, especially in individuals with a family history of diabetes, presumably because of preexisting impairment of insulin secretion. Cystic fibrosis, chronic pancreatitis, and hemochromatosis are examples of such problems, as is pancreatic insufficiency caused by trauma or surgical extirpation. These patients generally require insulin treatment. Also, they have glucagon deficiency due to decreased pancreatic α-cell mass and, thus, are prone to hypoglycemia. Excess glucagon, as seen in pancreatic glucagonomas, also may lead to increased insulin resistance and manifest as hyperglycemia.

DRUG-INDUCED DIABETES MELLITUS

A number of medications can cause hyperglycemia through a variety of mechanisms, including decreased insulin production and release, hepatic or peripheral insulin resistance, and increased hepatic glucose production (12). For example, corticosteroids are well known to cause hyperglycemia, and even to precipitate ketoacidosis. The relative risk of developing new-onset diabetes is dose related and ranges from 1.8 at less than 10 mg/d of prednisone to 10.3 with doses in excess of 30 mg/d of prednisone (13). Protease inhibitors are known to cause diabetes, but the likelihood is probably less than 1%. Although β-blockers may reduce insulin sensitivity, it would be rare for them to produce new-onset diabetes mellitus. Thiazide diuretics may cause hypokalemia, which in turn can lead to decreased insulin secretion. This is not a common cause of diabetes mellitus. A number of studies have demonstrated an increased risk of diabetes mellitus among individuals who use statins, with relative risks generally in the 1.09–1.15 range (14). However, a recent thoughtful review concluded that the benefits of taking statins to prevent CV disease probably outweigh any risks of developing new-onset diabetes (14). Cyclosporine and, to a likely greater extent, tacrolimus are associated with posttransplantation diabetes; absolute risk estimates range from less than 5% to more than 30% and are almost certainly confounded by other risk factors likely to be present in transplant recipients. Clozapine, one of the atypical antidepressants, has been associated with the development of diabetes in 1–30% of treated patients.

ENDOCRINE DISORDERS

A number of endocrinopathies involve diabetes mellitus. These conditions have in common an excess of hormones that are insulin antagonists, such as cortisol, glucagon, growth hormone, and epinephrine. Among the endocrine disorders are Cushing syndrome, acromegaly, glucagonoma, and pheochromocytoma.

GESTATIONAL DIABETES MELLITUS

Gestational diabetes mellitus is carbohydrate intolerance of varying severity with onset or first recognition during pregnancy. Pregnancy hormones induce a state of insulin resistance in all pregnant women, but most women can increase insulin production and maintain euglycemia. Women with preexisting insulin secretory defects or perhaps with preexisting reduced insulin

sensitivity are unable to produce and release enough extra
insulin to maintain circulating glucose at normal levels, and
they develop GDM. Gestational diabetes mellitus is a marker for
the subsequent development of diabetes mellitus, and, in some
cases, preexisting diabetes mellitus may have been undiagnosed
before pregnancy. Gestational diabetes mellitus will be discussed
in greater detail later in this monograph.

Epidemiology

A useful general concept is that the closer to the Equator a population lives, the greater the likelihood of type 2 diabetes mellitus
in this population; the further from the Equator, the greater the
likelihood of type 1 diabetes mellitus. For example, Scandinavian countries tend to have much more type 1 diabetes mellitus,
whereas countries, such as Italy and Spain, experience higher
prevalence of type 2 diabetes mellitus. Of course, recent trends
in immigration and relocation have changed these statistics con-
siderably; the Scandinavian countries are experiencing marked
increases in type 2 diabetes mellitus in their nonnative populations. The Pima population of Arizona and New Mexico has the
highest prevalence of type 2 diabetes mellitus in the world, and
evidence exists that this is a recent development for this group,
with low rates of type 2 diabetes mellitus recorded in surveys a
century ago (15). It has been postulated that the lifestyle tran-
sition from a hunter–gatherer existence to a more sedentary
western lifestyle led to an increase in obesity superimposed on
a genetic predisposition to diabetes mellitus. That predisposition
often is described as the "thrifty genotype." When food supplies
are intermittent, with starvation alternating with times of plenty,
it is advantageous to be able to store energy as fat to prepare
for famine, and so this genotype evolved. However, this same
genotype may confer a propensity to obesity and, thus, diabetes
when diet and lifestyle changes occur and famine is no longer
an ever-present possibility. Currently, more than 50% of Pimas
have diabetes and most are obese (15). Similarly, as the natives
of many Arab countries have transitioned from nomadic to more
sedentary lifestyles, the prevalence of obesity and type 2 diabetes
mellitus has increased significantly.

TYPE 1 DIABETES MELLITUS

Gender differences in the prevalence of diabetes mellitus are best understood if stratified by type of diabetes, age, and geographic region. Most autoimmune diseases occur more frequently in females than in males. Type 1 diabetes mellitus seems to be an exception (16). In individuals younger than 15 years, a slight male preponderance exists in Europeans and possibly a female excess in Asia and Africa. Populations with a high overall incidence of type 1 diabetes mellitus have a male excess, whereas populations with little type 1 diabetes mellitus are female predominant. In young adults, a consistent male preponderance exists. In adult and older age groups, type 1 diabetes mellitus shifts away from an almost exclusively autoimmune pathophysiology and merges with type 2 diabetes mellitus. Many individuals with type 2 diabetes mellitus gradually develop insulinopenia and may be reclassified. It is more difficult to distinguish type 1 diabetes mellitus from type 2 diabetes mellitus in older individuals, so epidemiologic studies are more difficult.

Offspring of men with type 1 diabetes mellitus are twice as likely to develop type 1 diabetes mellitus as offspring of women with type 1 diabetes mellitus (17). Offspring of older nondiabetic women are more likely to develop type 1 diabetes mellitus than offspring of younger healthy women (17). Both of these phenomena are the subject of current investigations, but no explanation has been confirmed at this time.

TYPE 2 DIABETES MELLITUS

In 2010, 11.8% of adult men (aged 20 years or older) and 10.8% of adult women had diagnosed or undiagnosed diabetes (1). Although a clear female preponderance existed for type 2 diabetes mellitus in the first half of the twentieth century in the United States and the United Kingdom, such gender difference is no longer reported (16). One potential explanation is that whereas obesity was formerly more common in women than in men, more recently, men appear to be developing obesity in proportions approaching those among women. According to the NHANES data, the prevalence of overweight (defined as a body mass index [BMI] of 27.3 [calculated as weight in kilograms divided by height in meters squared]) or more at the time among adult men (aged 20 years and older) increased from 22.8% in 1960–1962 to 31.7% in 1988–1991 and, among adult women, from 25.7% to 34.9% (18). In 1998, the classifications of overweight and obesity were modified; overweight is now a BMI of 25–29.9 and obesity is a BMI of 30 or greater. In the 1999–2000 NHANES, 33.4% of adult women and 27.5% of adult men in the United States had a BMI of 30 or greater. In 2007–2008, the prevalence of obesity was 35.5% for women and 32.2% for men (19). Conversely, in 2007–2008, 72.3% of adult men and 64.1% of adult American women were overweight or obese (a BMI of 25 or greater). It appears that the trend of overweight and obesity has leveled off (20), but the presence of obesity in 35% of adults and of overweight and obesity in 69% of adults explains a great deal of the current epidemic of type 2 diabetes mellitus and also may explain the similar prevalence among men and women.

With respect to race and ethnicity, in 2010, 10.2% of adult non-Hispanic whites in the United States and 18.7% of adult non-Hispanic blacks had diagnosed or undiagnosed diabetes. Although data for undiagnosed diabetes were not available for all racial or ethnic groups, diagnosed diabetes was 18% higher among Asian Americans, 66% higher among Hispanics, and 77% higher among non-Hispanic blacks than among non-Hispanic whites in the 2007–2008 NHANES (19). On the Indian subcontinent, compared with other parts of the world, type 2 diabetes mellitus is less likely to be associated with obesity.

In the 2007–2008 NHANES data for women, 33% of non-Hispanic white adults, 49.6% of non-Hispanic blacks, and 43% of Hispanics were obese. As mentioned earlier, metabolic syndrome appears to be a major contributor to the epidemic of diabetes (19). In the 2003–2006 NHANES data, men were slightly more likely to manifest metabolic syndrome than women (35% compared with 33%), but this difference was not statistically significant (10). The prevalence of metabolic syndrome in women aged 40–59 years (37.2%) was more than double the prevalence of metabolic syndrome in women aged 20–39 years (15.6%). Among women older than 60 years, 54.4% met the criteria for metabolic syndrome. Non-Hispanic black and Mexican-American women were 1.5 times more likely to have metabolic syndrome than non-Hispanic white women. Increasing BMI was strongly associated with metabolic syndrome, as might be expected. Although only 9% of underweight or normal-weight women had at least three criteria for metabolic syndrome, the prevalence increased to 33% in overweight women and 56% in obese women.

Role of the Obstetrician–Gynecologist

Obstetrician–gynecologists often are the only health care providers consulted by women of reproductive age; therefore, they can play a key role in counseling patients regarding healthy lifestyles, which are critical for the prevention of diabetes mellitus. Also, obstetrician–gynecologists are in a position to identify patients with risk factors (Box 1) and to provide screening, early diagnosis, and appropriate management.

Prevention

Type 1 Diabetes Mellitus

Presently, no accepted paradigm for prevention of type 1 diabetes mellitus exists, although there is evidence that breastfeeding with later introduction of cow's milk may decrease the risk of children developing this condition. Early or late introduction of cereals that contain gluten or rice, before 4 months of age or after 6 months of age, was associated with development of islet antibodies in one study (21). An ongoing multinational randomized trial that compares standard cow's milk formula with a highly hydrolyzed casein formula recruited more than 2,000 infants from 15 countries (22). The infants are at a high risk of type 1 diabetes mellitus and the trial seeks to establish whether weaning to a highly hydrolyzed formula in infancy subsequently reduces the risk of type 1 diabetes mellitus. The results are expected sometime after 2017. Until further data become available, it is clear that the overall benefits of breastfeeding are positive and all women, including those with type 1 diabetes mellitus, should be encouraged to do so.

Type 2 Diabetes Mellitus

Box 1 lists risk factors for type 2 diabetes mellitus. Patients with these risk factors should be tested (see the section "Screening and Diagnosis") and those with prediabetes should be counseled that intervention can decrease the risk of developing type 2 diabetes mellitus. A randomized trial, the Diabetes Prevention Program,

 Box 1. Risk Factors for Type 2 Diabetes Mellitus

Patients with a body mass index of 25 or more (calculated as weight in kilograms divided by height in meters squared) plus the following risk factors should be tested for type 2 diabetes mellitus:

☑ Physical inactivity

☑ First-degree relative with diabetes mellitus

☑ Race or ethnicity with high prevalence of diabetes mellitus

☑ History of gestational diabetes mellitus or giving birth to a macrosomic infant

☑ Hypertension

☑ Low high-density lipoprotein cholesterol level (less than 35 mg/dL) or high triglyceride level (more than 250 mg/dL)

☑ Polycystic ovary syndrome

☑ Previous prediabetes

☑ Evidence of insulin resistance

Otherwise, testing should begin at age 45 years and repeated every 3 years unless risk factors dictate more frequent testing.

Based on data from Standards of medical care in diabetes--2012. American Diabetes Association. Diabetes Care 2012;35 Suppl 1:S11–63.

demonstrated conclusively that preventive measures can significantly reduce the likelihood of developing diabetes mellitus (23). During the 2.8-year study period, diabetes developed at a rate of 11 per 100 person-years in the control group of participants randomized to receive placebo; those who received metformin, 850 mg twice daily, developed diabetes at a rate of 7.8 per 100 person-years, a 31% reduction. The third arm of the study involved lifestyle modification designed to achieve at least a 7% weight loss and included at least 150 minutes of physical activity per week. Diabetes developed in participants at a rate of 4.8 per 100 person-years, a 58% reduction from the control group. The number of participants needed to treat with lifestyle intervention for 3 years to prevent one case of diabetes was 6.9. A number of other trials around the world have reported similar results. At least one nationwide effort has been mounted by the YMCA to translate the Diabetes Prevention Program lifestyle intervention approach into a practical program to help individuals at risk of developing diabetes. Information regarding the location of programs is available at http://www.ymca.net/diabetes-prevention.

The American Diabetes Association (ADA) recommends the following strategies for physicians who provide care for patients with prediabetes (see the section "Screening and Diagnosis") (3):

- Refer patients to an "effective ongoing support program targeting weight loss of 7% of body weight and increasing physical activity to at least 150 minutes per week of moderate activity, such as walking."

- Consider metformin therapy for those at highest risk, such as patients with multiple risk factors whose hyperglycemia progresses (eg, mean hemoglobin A_{1c} [HbA_{1c}] level exceeds 6%) despite lifestyle intervention

- Monitor for the development of diabetes mellitus annually

- Provide follow-up counseling; it appears to be important for successful prevention of diabetes mellitus

The Diabetes Reduction Assessment With Ramipril and Rosiglitazone Medication (or DREAM Trial), a randomized trial of rosiglitazone versus placebo for patients with prediabetes (24), demonstrated a dramatic reduction in diabetes mellitus over

3 years (10% versus 26%); however, an apparent increased risk of myocardial infarction resulted in the U.S. Food and Drug Administration (FDA) markedly restricting the availability of this drug. Primary prevention of type 2 diabetes mellitus is not currently an approved use for rosiglitazone.

 CASE NO. 1. A 35-year-old Mexican-American woman comes in for her annual gynecologic examination. Her BMI is 38, and she mentions that her last child weighed 4,500 g at birth.

This patient has at least two risk factors for type 2 diabetes. She should be tested for diabetes with either a fasting plasma glucose test, an HbA_{1c} test, or a 75-g oral glucose tolerance test (OGTT) (Table 1). If the results are diagnostic of prediabetes, she should be counseled about the risks of type 2 diabetes mellitus and the need for lifestyle modification aimed at a weight loss of at least 7% of body weight and including at least 150 minutes per week of moderate physical activity. She should be referred to a program, such as one offered at many YMCA centers, to provide motivation and guidance, and she should be tested for diabetes mellitus annually.

Screening and Diagnosis

Ordinarily, screening tests are applied to identify individuals at high risk of the disease in question, who should subsequently undergo the diagnostic test. With diabetes mellitus, the screening test and the diagnostic test are generally identical, unless one considers obtaining a medical history as a screening test. Therefore, in this monograph, "testing for diabetes" will be used rather than "screening." Signs and symptoms of diabetes mellitus are listed in Box 2. Although type 1 diabetes mellitus usually presents acutely with clinically evident symptoms and marked hyperglycemia, it is possible to identify some at-risk patients by testing for islet autoantibodies. Because type 1 diabetes mellitus is less common than type 2 diabetes mellitus, widespread autoantibody screening programs would not be cost effective. It is not clear at this time whether intervention could prevent the development of

Table 1. Diagnostic Criteria for Diabetes and Prediabetes

| Marker* | Diabetes | Prediabetes | |
		Impaired Fasting Glucose	Impaired Glucose Tolerance
Fasting plasma glucose level	126 mg/dL or more	100–125 mg/dL	N/A
2-hour plasma glucose on 75-g oral glucose tolerance test	200 mg/dL or more	N/A	140–199 mg/dL
Hemoglobin A$_{1c}$ level (certified by the National Glycohemoglobin Standardization Program and standardized to the methods of the Diabetes Control and Complications Trial)	6.5% or more	5.7–6.4%	
Random plasma glucose level in symptomatic patient	200 mg/dL or more	N/A	

*Positive results should be confirmed by repeat testing unless the diagnosis of diabetes is clinically unequivocal. It should be noted that test strips and reflectance meters are not precise or accurate enough for diagnostic testing. Measurement of plasma glucose levels should be performed by a qualified clinical laboratory. If serum samples are used, care should be taken to ice the specimen as soon as possible and to separate serum from red blood cells immediately in order to avoid artificially low results caused by glycolysis by red blood cells. Therefore, plasma glucose level measurement is preferred.

Data from Standards of medical care in diabetes--2012. American Diabetes Association. Diabetes Care 2012;35 Suppl 1:S11–63.

type 1 diabetes mellitus in individuals with autoantibodies. The diagnostic criteria for diabetes mellitus are the same for all types.

Type 2 diabetes mellitus most often is present for a long time, often years, before any symptoms are noted by the patient. Complications may have already occurred when symptoms are present. That is why testing based on risk factors is so important. Risk factors for type 2 diabetes mellitus, along with recommendations for testing, are listed in Box 1. The diagnosis of diabetes or prediabetes may be established in a number of ways, including

---

Box 2. Signs and Symptoms of Diabetes Mellitus

- Unusual thirst
- Extreme hunger
- Excessive urination
- Weight loss
- Extreme fatigue or irritability
- Nausea
- Blurred vision
- Sores, cuts, and bruises that are slow to heal
- Recurrent infections, particularly of the vagina, gums, bladder, or skin
- Numbness or tingling in the feet or hands
- Irregular menstruation

---

with an HbA_{1c} test, a fasting plasma glucose test, a 2-hour 75-g OGTT, or evidence of an unequivocally elevated random plasma glucose level in a symptomatic patient. Diagnostic thresholds are shown in Table 1. The use of HbA_{1c} to diagnose diabetes was adopted by the ADA in 2010 based on data that showed a similar relationship between HbA_{1c} and diabetic vascular disease as for fasting and 2-hour plasma glucose. An HbA_{1c} test has practical advantages, including the fact that no particular preparation is needed, and a single blood sample is all that is necessary. The assay should be performed in a laboratory that uses a method that is certified by the National Glycohemoglobin Standardization Program and standardized to the Diabetes Control and Complications Trial reference assay. Point-of-care assays are not accurate enough for diagnosis. An HbA_{1c} test will detect fewer cases of diabetes than will plasma glucose-based tests, but the convenience and patient acceptability make it a practical test. Particular assay methodologies should be used when patients have variant hemoglobins, such as sickle cell trait; when the red blood cell turnover is not normal, glucose criteria should be used. Generally, it is recommended that any test with a positive result be repeated in order to rule out laboratory error, unless the clinical diagnosis is unequivocal.

The diagnosis of prediabetes, including HbA_{1c} level of 5.7–6.4%, impaired fasting glucose, and impaired glucose tolerance, should be considered to impart a continuum of risk. The likelihood of developing diabetes within 5 years was 25–50% when HbA_{1c} level was 6–6.5%, 9–25% at HbA_{1c} level of 5.5–6%, and less than 9% at HbA_{1c} level of 5–5.5% (25). Patients with prediabetes should be counseled regarding their increased risk of diabetes mellitus and CV disease and the use of strategies to decrease these risks as outlined earlier. Referral to support programs that emphasize intensive lifestyle modification with weight reduction and physical activity is critically important; such programs are effective in preventing progression to diabetes (23).

Management

Establishing a dialogue with the patient early in the course of her treatment is critical. Suggestions for the content of that discussion are outlined in Box 3.

The Health Care Team

The successful management of diabetes mellitus requires the physician to coordinate a team of professionals, including physicians, diabetes nurse educators, physician's assistants or nurse practitioners, nurses, dietitians, pharmacists, and mental health professionals with competence and special interest in diabetes. Often team members have the expertise and interest to fulfill more than one of those roles. Foot care specialists and medical subspecialists often will supplement the team. Obstetricians with special expertise and interest in diabetic pregnancy and neonatologists should be coordinating care of a pregnant woman with diabetes and her infant. The patient is at the center of the team and must take primary responsibility for her health and well-being. The ADA's standards of care state (26): "Implementation of the management plan requires that each aspect is understood

Box 3. Counseling Patients With Diabetes Mellitus: Establishing a Dialogue

- Describe the diabetes mellitus disease process and treatment options
- Outline the roles of each member of the management team
- Describe the management plan
- Provide information regarding the importance of nutrition and healthy diet
- Emphasize lifestyle modifications, as appropriate:
  —Smoking cessation
  —Physical activity and diet
- Outline goals for achieving or maintaining a healthy body weight
- Discuss medications, if appropriate
- Discuss a need for and goals of self-monitoring of glucose and hemoglobin A_{1c} levels
- Describe the importance of prevention, detection, and treatment of acute and chronic complications
- Recommend daily self-examination of feet to prevent ingrown toenails, corns, and calluses
- Emphasize importance of regular physical examinations
- Discuss psychosocial adjustments to daily life with diabetes mellitus
- Outline goals of preconception care and pregnancy management, if appropriate

and agreed to by the patient and the care providers and that the goals and treatment plan are reasonable. Any plan should recognize diabetes self-management education and ongoing diabetes support as an integral component of care. In developing the plan, consideration should be given to the patient's age, school or work schedule and conditions, physical activity, eating patterns, social situation and cultural factors, and presence of complications of diabetes or other medical conditions." National standards for diabetes self-management education outline the components of quality patient education (27). The health care team should include one or more educators who use these standards. Sometimes it is in the best interest of the patient to refer her so that an appropriate team can provide the care.

Initial Evaluation

When diabetes is newly diagnosed, or a patient is newly referred, a complete medical evaluation should be performed. The goals of this evaluation are to classify the diabetes, detect complications of the disease, construct a management plan, and review previous management if the diagnosis is not new. The initial evaluation should include obtaining of a medical history with attention to the circumstances of the onset and diagnosis of diabetes, the patient's current nutritional and physical activity patterns, previous treatment regimens, and current treatment. Current medications should be noted, and the patient should be asked about hyperglycemia and hypoglycemia symptoms. A history of microvascular and macrovascular complications should be obtained. Cardiovascular risk factors should be documented. For women in the reproductive years, family planning should be discussed. The physical examination should include a review of vital signs, including measured weight and height with calculation of BMI. Special emphasis should be placed on documenting evidence of diabetic complications, including a careful foot examination, skin examination for acanthosis nigricans, and dilated optic fundus examination (typically by an ophthalmologist with expertise in the retina). Thyromegaly should be sought. Laboratory testing should include HbA_{1c} level measurement, lipid profile, liver function tests, measurement of urinary protein excretion, and serum creatinine level measurement. Referrals should be made for dental examination, nutritional counseling, and diabetes self-management education. When appropriate, consultation from a mental health professional and ophthalmologist should be considered.

Medical Nutrition Therapy

Patients with diabetes mellitus or prediabetes should receive nutrition counseling, preferably from a registered dietitian with expertise in diabetes nutrition. As for other aspects of the diabetes management plan, medical nutrition therapy counseling should take into consideration the patient's lifestyle, cultural needs, and social needs. It is obvious that certain lifestyle modifications are likely necessary for successful diabetes management. Recommendations from the ADA are outlined in Box 4. A number of other specific suggestions may be found in the ADA's position statement "Nutrition Recommendations and Interventions for Diabetes" (28).

Exercise Therapy

Physical activity should be combined with medical nutrition therapy in the treatment plan. Regular exercise may prevent type 2 diabetes mellitus in individuals at risk (23). Exercise programs that lasted at least 8 weeks decreased HbA_{1c} levels by 0.66%, on average, in individuals with type 2 diabetes even when BMI remained unchanged (29). The greater the exercise intensity, the greater the decrease in HbA_{1c} levels. The ADA recommends that individuals with diabetes mellitus perform at least 150 minutes per week of moderate intensity aerobic physical activity (50–70% of maximum heart rate) and, in the absence of contraindications, perform resistance training three times per week (26). These recommendations are consistent with those of the U.S. Department of Health and Human Services for all Americans older than 18 years, which recommend 150 minutes per week of moderate intensity or 75 minutes per week of vigorous aerobic physical activity (30). The U.S. Department of Health and Human Services also recommends that adults perform muscle strengthening activities that involve all major muscle groups on two or more days per week. The American Diabetes Association recommends that patients with diabetes be assessed for conditions that might contraindicate exercise or predispose to injury, such as uncontrolled hypertension, severe autonomic neuropathy, severe peripheral neuropathy or history of foot lesions, and unstable proliferative retinopathy (26). Clinical judgment should be used in assessing patients with multiple risk factors for coronary artery disease, and high-risk patients should increase the intensity and duration of exercise gradually.

Box 4. Medical Nutrition Therapy Recommendations

Goals

- Achieve and maintain blood glucose levels in the normal range or as close to normal as safely possible
- Achieve and maintain lipid and lipoprotein profiles that reduce the risk of vascular disease
- Achieve and maintain blood pressure levels in the normal range or as close to normal as safely possible
- Prevent or slow the rate of development of chronic complications of diabetes mellitus
- Take into account personal and cultural preferences and willingness to change
- Maintain the pleasure of eating by limiting food choices only when indicated by scientific evidence

Overweight and Obesity

- For weight loss, low-carbohydrate or low-fat calorie restricted diets may be effective in the short term (up to 1 year).
- Physical activity and behavior modification are most helpful in maintenance of weight loss.
- Weight loss medications may be considered in the treatment of overweight and obese individuals with type 2 diabetes mellitus. Bariatric surgery may be considered for some individuals with type 2 diabetes mellitus and a body mass index of 35 or more (calculated as weight in kilograms divided by height in meters squared).

(continued)

Box 4. Medical Nutrition Therapy Recommendations *(continued)*

Carbohydrate Intake

- Monitoring carbohydrate intake is a key strategy.
- Use of the glycemic index may provide a modest additional benefit.
- Sugar alcohols and nonnutritive sweeteners are safe when consumed within the daily intake levels established by the U.S. Food and Drug Administration.

Fat Intake

- Limit saturated fat intake to less than 7% of total calories
- Minimize intake of trans fat
- Limit dietary cholesterol intake to less than 200 mg/d
- Ensure intake of omega-3 polyunsaturated fatty acids by consuming two or more servings of fish per week

Protein

- The usual protein intake (15–20% of energy) need not be modified when renal function is normal
- With type 2 diabetes mellitus, ingested protein can increase insulin response without increasing plasma glucose concentrations. Therefore, protein should not be used to treat acute or prevent nighttime hypoglycemia.
- High-protein diets are not recommended as a method for weight loss.

Based on data from Bantle JP, Wylie-Rosett J, Albright AL, Apovian CM, Clark NG, Franz MJ, et al. Nutrition recommendations and interventions for diabetes: a position statement of the American Diabetes Association. American Diabetes Association [published erratum appears in Diabetes Care 2010;33:1911]. Diabetes Care 2008;31 Suppl 1:S61–78.

Evaluating Glucose Control

One of the most important components of the management plan for diabetes is the setting of goals for glycemic control and the evaluation of progress toward those goals. The ADA considers an HbA_{1c} level less than 7% to be a reasonable goal for many nonpregnant adults (26). Attainment of such a goal has been demonstrated to reduce microvascular and neuropathic complications of type 1 diabetes mellitus and type 2 diabetes mellitus (31, 32). A beneficial effect on CV disease has been harder to demonstrate, and results of various studies are conflicting. However, long-term follow-up studies in which patients started intensive glycemic control early in the course of their diabetes, when the likelihood of established coronary disease is low, have demonstrated benefit (33). Conversely, individuals with longstanding type 2 diabetes mellitus and preexisting coronary disease may be at a greater risk of CV disease with the rapid institution of tight glycemic control (34). Therefore, the ADA recommends that less stringent HbA_{1c} goals may be considered for individuals with longstanding diabetes in whom the usual goal is difficult to attain and for those with a history of severe hypoglycemia, limited life expectancy, advanced microvascular or macrovascular complications, or extensive comorbid conditions (26).

Hemoglobin A_{1c} levels, which reflect average blood glucose levels over the previous 2–3 months, have been shown to correlate well with mean plasma glucose values in a large trial of adults with and without diabetes mellitus (35). In order to improve patients' understanding of HbA_{1c} values and goals, it is helpful to report results as the HbA_{1c} percentage and as the estimated average glucose level. The relationship between HbA_{1c} and the estimated average glucose level is linear; an HbA_{1c} value of 6% reflects an estimated average glucose level of 126 mg/dL and an HbA_{1c} value of 10% correlates with an estimated average glucose level of 240 mg/dL. An online calculator is available at http://professional.diabetes.org/GlucoseCalculator.aspx. Hemoglobin A_{1c} converter applications also are available free or at a nominal price for smartphones and similar devices.

Goals for glycemic control, which are recommended by the ADA, are shown in Table 2. The goals were based on achieving HbA_{1c} values less than 7%, as noted earlier. It should be noted

Table 2. Goals for Glycemic Control for Nonpregnant Adults with Diabetes*

Marker	Level
Hemoglobin A_{1c}	Less than 7%
Preprandial capillary plasma glucose	70–130 mg/dL
Peak postprandial capillary plasma glucose	Less than 180 mg/dL

*Goals should be individualized based on the following factors:
• Duration of diabetes
• Age and life expectancy
• Comorbid conditions
• Known cardiovascular disease or advanced microvascular complications
• Hypoglycemia unawareness
• Individual patient considerations

More or less stringent goals may be appropriate for individual patients. Improvement in postprandial glucose levels may be targeted if hemoglobin A_{1c} goals are not met despite reaching preprandial glucose goals.
Data from Standards of medical care in diabetes--2012. American Diabetes Association. Diabetes Care 2012;35 Suppl 1:S11–63.

that goals may be modified based on a number of individual patient factors that can make intensive glycemic control difficult to achieve or lack benefit in that individual. Goals for glycemic control in pregnant women with diabetes mellitus or GDM will be discussed later in this monograph. The timing of self-glucose monitoring is somewhat controversial. Randomized trials, such as the United Kingdom Prospective Diabetes Study Group (32), used preprandial testing to determine the importance of glycemic control to prevent complications in participants with type 2 diabetes mellitus. However, evidence exists that postprandial hyperglycemia is an independent risk factor for CV disease (36). Many health care providers advise patients to monitor their glucose levels before each meal. The ADA advises that when HbA_{1c} targets are not reached once goals for fasting and preprandial glucose are met, postprandial glucose testing (1–2 hours after meals) aimed at reducing postprandial values to less than 180 mg/dL may help reduce HbA_{1c} levels (26).

Pharmacologic Therapy

INSULIN FOR TYPE 1 DIABETES MELLITUS

Type 1 diabetes mellitus is treated with insulin, which is administered subcutaneously as replacement therapy. Insulin also may be used by some patients with type 2 diabetes mellitus when other modes of treatment are inadequate to achieve goals. This is particularly an issue with longstanding type 2 diabetes mellitus when pancreatic reserve may be exhausted.

Mechanism of Action. Insulin is a peptide hormone composed of 51 amino acids in two chains that are held together by disulfide bonds. The β-cells of the islets of Langerhans in the pancreas produce insulin in the form of proinsulin, which contains the A chains and B chains described earlier that are connected by a C chain. The C chain, also called C-peptide or connecting peptide, is cleaved and released into the circulation in equimolar amounts to insulin. Exogenously administered insulin does not contain C-peptide. Insulin acts at many sites throughout the body. This hormone is one of the main factors responsible for maintaining euglycemia (normal circulating glucose levels). It allows glucose to be transported into muscle and adipocytes. Insulin allows glucose to be stored in the liver as glycogen, and when insulin levels are low, the glycogen is converted back to glucose, which is released into the circulation to restore euglycemia. Insulin also favors the creation, in adipocytes, of triglycerides from free fatty acids and glycerol. When insulin is lacking, triglycerides are broken down and free fatty acids are released into the circulation. They are transported to the liver and broken down to ketone bodies, which can cause diabetic ketoacidosis. Insulin has many other effects, which are beyond the scope of this monograph.

Types of Insulin. Exogenous insulin is now produced by recombinant DNA methodology, typically using plants or bacteria, such as *Escherichia coli*, into which the insulin gene has been transferred. Many different kinds of insulin are available; they differ in one of two ways: 1) some types of insulin, such as neutral protamine Hagedorn, consist of human insulin with substances added to delay the absorption and prolong the action after subcutaneous injection and 2) newer insulin analogues substitute one or more amino acids in the insulin chain. This may hasten the absorption and shorten the duration of action of the insulin, as in insulin lispro and insulin aspart, or it may prolong the action and abolish the absorption peak, as in insulin glargine and insulin detemir. This allows for greater flexibility, especially in the treatment of type 1 diabetes mellitus. Insulin also is used for the treatment of type 2 diabetes mellitus in some patients for whom other treatments are ineffective, and it is the standard of care for the management of preexisting type 1 diabetes mellitus and type 2 diabetes mellitus in pregnancy. It is commonly used for the treatment of GDM when medical nutritional therapy is not sufficient to maintain euglycemia. Table 3 lists information about the different types of insulin that are available.

Delivery Systems. Insulin is administered subcutaneously. Insulin in a concentration of 100 units per milliliter (U-100) usually is dispensed in vials that contain 10 mL. Insulin syringes are available in 0.5-mL and 1-mL sizes. The 0.5-mL syringes are calibrated in 1-unit increments, and the 1-mL syringes are calibrated in 2-unit increments. Insulin vials can be kept at room temperature for up to 6 weeks or in a refrigerator (not a freezer) until the expiration date. Some patients with type 2 diabetes mellitus will require more than 100 units of insulin at a time. One manufacturer

Table 3. Characteristics of Various Insulin Preparations

Preparation	Onset of Action	Peak of Action	Duration of Effect
Human Insulin Preparations			
Short-acting regular crystalline zinc insulin	30–60 minutes	2–4 hours	6–12 hours
Intermediate-acting neutral protamine Hagedorn	1–2 hours	4–14 hours	10–24 hours
Rapid-Acting Analogs			
Insulin lispro	Less than 30 minutes	30–90 minutes	Less than 6 hours
Insulin aspart	Less than 15 minutes	1–3 hours	3–5 hours
Insulin glulisine	Less than 30 minutes	30–90 minutes	Less than 6 hours
Long-Acting Analogs*			
Insulin detemir	1 hour	No peak	6–23 hours
Insulin glargine	1 hour	No peak	24 hours

*Long-acting analogs should not be mixed in the same syringe with other types of insulin.

produces regular insulin in a concentration of 500 units per milliliter (U-500). To distinguish this highly concentrated insulin from the usual U-100 insulin, it is packaged in 20-mL vials that have brown stripes on the label. Because syringes to satisfy administration of U-500 insulin do not exist, great care must be exercised to ensure that patients are using U-500 insulin correctly. Each unit marked on the U-100 syringe actually translates to 5 units of U-500 insulin. Currently, neither neutral protamine Hagedorn insulin nor any of the insulin analogs are available in any concentration other than U-100.

Pharmaceutical companies also market various types of insulin in disposable "pens" with which the patient can dial in a particular dose and inject herself without drawing up insulin from a vial. Some of the pens contain intermediate-acting and short-acting types of insulin in fixed proportions (50:50, 70:30, or 75:25). Use of such pens adds convenience but limits the flexibility in dosage proportions that is sometimes helpful.

Continuous subcutaneous insulin infusion pumps provide a system to mimic the basal insulin release from the normal pancreas, interspersed with bolus doses after meals. Although insulin pumps have not clearly demonstrated improved outcomes compared with intensive conventional insulin therapy, they provide increased flexibility by allowing greater variation in timing of meals and the ability to program changes in the basal insulin infusion rate at particular times of day. Some studies have demonstrated a reduction in hypoglycemic episodes with continuous subcutaneous insulin infusion pump therapy (37). The ADA makes the following recommendations for the pharmacologic management of type 1 diabetes mellitus (26):

- Use multiple-dose injections (three to four injections per day of basal and prandial insulin) or continuous subcutaneous insulin infusion therapy
- Match prandial insulin to carbohydrate intake, preprandial blood glucose, and anticipated activity
- Use insulin analogs, especially if hypoglycemia is a problem

A review of data regarding various approaches to insulin therapy for type 1 diabetes mellitus and type 2 diabetes mellitus provides helpful information (38). Practical advice, particularly for the treatment of individuals with type 2 diabetes mellitus who require insulin, also is available (39).

TREATMENT OF TYPE 2 DIABETES MELLITUS

A number of treatment options are available for patients with type 2 diabetes mellitus. Beginning in 2006, algorithms were published as a result of consensus between representatives of the ADA and the European Association for the Study of Diabetes. The most recent update of those recommendations was published in 2009 (40). These recommendations, which are updated every few years as more data become available, are a useful guide to management. They embrace the goal of HbA_{1c} value less than 7% in most cases, with the possibility of individualization when specific risk factors are present or absent. Antidiabetic agents are selected based on their effectiveness in decreasing glucose levels (as reflected by HbA_{1c} levels), safety profiles, adverse effects, tolerability, ease of use, and expense. The recommended order of therapy is as follows:

1. Decrease weight and increase activity (expected HbA_{1c} level decrease, 1–2%)

2. Add metformin (expected HbA_{1c} level decrease, 1–2%)

3. If needed, add therapy with insulin or a sulfonylurea (expected HbA_{1c} level decrease, 1–3.5%)

4. If needed, add therapy with thiazolidinedione or glucagon-like peptide-1 agonist (less well-validated, expected HbA_{1c} level decrease, 0.5–1.4%)

5. Other agents may be introduced; all are expensive and not well-validated

The mechanism of action and dosages of various antidiabetic drugs are outlined in Table 4 and described in the following paragraphs.

Insulin Secretogogues. Sulfonylureas are oral agents that bind to sulfonylurea receptors in β-cells, thereby increasing sensitivity to glucose and other secretogogues, such as certain amino acids and increasing insulin secretion at all blood glucose levels.

Table 4. Characteristics of Medications Used to Treat Type 2 Diabet

Group of Medication	Route	Preparations
		Sec
Sulfonylureas	Oral	Glyburide
		Glipizide
		Glimepiride
Meglitinides	Oral	Repaglinide
		Nateglinide
		Ins
Biguanides	Oral	Metformin
		Metformin (24 hours)
Thiazolidinediones	Oral	Rosiglitazone*
		Pioglitazone
		Increti
Glucagon-like peptide-1 analogs	Subcutaneous	Exenatide
		Liraglutide
		Exenatide, long-acting release
Dipeptidyl peptidase 4 inhibitors	Oral	Sitagliptin
		Saxagliptin
		Linagliptin
Alpha-glucosidase inhibitors	Oral	Acarbose
		Miglitol
Amylin analogs	Subcutaneous	Pramlintide

*Prescribing is restricted by the U.S. Food and Drug Administration.

In order for sulfonylureas to be effective, the patient must have residual β-cell function. Their major adverse effect is hypoglycemia. Weight gain also is reported, presumably because glucose is used more effectively when hyperglycemia is controlled. Second-generation sulfonylureas, such as glyburide and glipizide, are more potent on a weight basis and have a longer duration of action

ellitus

Duration of Action	Dosage	Adverse Effects

ues

Duration of Action	Dosage	Adverse Effects
20 hours	Twice a day	Hypoglycemia and weight gain with all secretogogues
10 hours	Daily or twice a day	
24 hours	Daily	
4–6 hours	Before meals	
4 hours	Before meals	

sitizers

Duration of Action	Dosage	Adverse Effects
Weeks (peak, 2–3 hours)	Daily to three times a day before meals	Transient gastrointestinal upset
Weeks (peak, 7 hours)	Daily	Possible lactic acidosis
Weeks (peak, 1 hour)	Daily or twice a day	Potential cardiovascular risk
Weeks (peak, 2 hours)	Daily	

ased Agents

Duration of Action	Dosage	Adverse Effects
Rapid onset; half-life, 2.4 hours	Twice a day before meals	Nausea, thyroid cancer risk, and pancreatitis with all three agents
Half-life, 13 hours (peak, 8–12 hours)	Daily Once a week	
Half-life, 12 hours (peak, 1–4 hours)	Daily	Too early to tell with all three agents
24 hours (peak, 2 hours)	Daily	
Half-life, 12 hours (peak, 1.5 hours)	Daily	
Not absorbed; local gastrointestinal half-life, 2 hours (peak, 2–3 hours)	Twice a day	Flatulence with both agents
Half-life, 2 hours (peak, 2–3 hours)	Twice a day	
3 hours (peak, 20 minutes)	Twice a day before meals	Nausea

than first-generation sulfonylureas, such as tolbutamide and chlor-propamide. Patients may become less sensitive to sulfonylureas over time. Sulfonylureas and meglitinides often are prescribed as monotherapy but also may be combined with other oral agents, such as metformin or thiazolidinediones. They may be combined with insulin as well. Glipizide is a short-acting sulfonylurea, with duration of action of approximately 14 hours. The usual dosage is 2.5–20 mg/d in two divided doses. Glyburide, also called gliben-clamide in Europe, may be given once a day or twice daily. The usual starting dosage is 2.5–5 mg/d, and the dosage is titrated to a maximum of 20 mg/d. Elderly patients or those who are highly sensitive may start with 1.25 mg/d. Glyburide is more likely to be associated with hypoglycemia than some of the other sulfo-nylureas. Glimepiride generally is given as a single daily dosage, starting at 1–2 mg/d and up to a maximum of 4 mg/d or, in some cases, 8 mg/d.

Meglitinides, such as repaglinide and nateglinide, act like the sulfonylureas but on a different receptor. They have a shorter effect than sulfonylureas and provide some flexibility because they are taken before meals. They may be useful in patients who are allergic to sulfonylureas. Repaglinide is taken before each meal, starting at 0.5 mg and titrating to a maximum of 4 mg. Nateglinide is taken at a dose of 60–120 mg before each meal.

Insulin Sensitizers. Metformin is the only available biguanide. It enhances the action of insulin on the liver by favoring glycogen formation and decreasing hepatic glucose output. Also, it increases insulin sensitivity in peripheral tissues, such as muscle, by favor-ing glucose use. It enhances insulin's action on adipocytes by increasing the formation of triglycerides and decreasing the release of free fatty acids. Metformin works only when insulin is present. Metformin is unlikely to cause hypoglycemia and may foster a modest reduction in weight. An adverse effect is gastroin-testinal (GI) upset that tends to be transient. An earlier biguanide, phenformin, was removed from the market because of frequent reports of lactic acidosis, sometimes fatal. Also, metformin has been associated with lactic acidosis, but less commonly (41). Risk factors for lactic acidosis include metformin overdose, renal impairment, and a history of lactic acidosis. Caution should be exercised in patients with renal compromise because of the pos-sibility of metformin accumulation.

Metformin also is used in the treatment of PCOS, which often is a component of the insulin resistance syndrome. Although other approaches are preferred for ovulation induction and for the treatment of hirsutism, metformin may be useful (42). The mechanism of action is not clear but is likely related to reduction in insulin resistance. When obese patients with insulin resistance syndrome have diabetes mellitus or prediabetes, metformin is a useful treatment, particularly because it often is associated with modest weight loss.

Metformin is marketed as tablets that contain 500 mg, 850 mg, and 1,000 mg of the agent. It is taken by mouth with meals. A usual starting dose is 500 mg or 850 mg with dinner or breakfast. If the initial dose is tolerated for 1–2 weeks, a second dose can be added at the other mealtime. Subsequently, the dose is slowly increased (every 1–2 weeks); many patients require 1,500–2,000 mg/d to achieve targets for glucose control. The maximum dose is 850 mg with each of the three meals. Metformin also is marketed in combination with sulfonylureas, thiazolidinediones, and dipeptidyl peptidase 4 inhibitors. A sustained release form of metformin that can be taken once per day also is available.

Rosiglitazone and pioglitazone are the orally active thiazolidinediones currently available in the United States. They act as agonists of the peroxisome proliferator-activated receptor gamma, found abundantly in adipose tissue. It is postulated that these drugs improve insulin sensitivity by increasing fatty acid uptake by adipose tissue. This decreases circulating fatty acid levels and decreases the adverse effect of free fatty acids on insulin-sensitive tissues, including muscle and the liver. Clinically, these drugs decrease both fasting and postprandial glucose levels and fatty acids. They improve hepatic insulin sensitivity and increase insulin-mediated glucose uptake in the periphery. Weight gain is a common adverse effect, presumably because of enhanced fat storage in adipocytes. On average, patients gain 2–3 kg (4.4–8.8 lb) of weight for every 1% decrease in HbA_{1c}. Some patients also retain excess fluid and experience peripheral edema. Congestive heart failure has been reported, especially in patients who took both thiazolidinediones and insulin (43). The first available thiazolidinedione, troglitazone, was removed from the market in 2000 because of reports of drug-induced hepatitis with elevated transaminase levels in approximately 2% of patients. The FDA estimated that acute liver failure occurred in approximately 1 per 1,000 person-years of exposure to the drug, with a number of reports of death or the need for liver transplant. However, hepatotoxicity appears to have been specific to troglitazone, and the agents currently available have not been associated with drug-induced hepatitis.

A 2007 meta-analysis found an increased risk of myocardial infarction and a nonstatistically significant increase in the risk of death from CV disease in patients who took rosiglitazone compared with those who took placebo or standard diabetes drugs (44). Although rates of CV risk have not been directly compared between users of rosiglitazone and users of pioglitazone, studies that involved pioglitazone have not reported an excess of myocardial events. The FDA restricted access to rosiglitazone in 2010. Patients who are already taking rosiglitazone may continue doing so if they appear to benefit from it and acknowledge the risks. Patients may be newly prescribed the drug only if they are unsuccessful in achieving glucose control with other medications and opt not to take pioglitazone for medical reasons. Prescribers of rosiglitazone and pharmacists filling prescriptions must be specifically certified.

The FDA issued a box warning that thiazolidinediones may cause or exacerbate heart failure and are contraindicated in patients with symptomatic heart failure. In addition, the FDA issued a special alert in 2011 of an ongoing safety review because of preliminary reports of an association between high doses and prolonged use of pioglitazone and bladder cancer, although no definitive answer is yet available. The FDA advises that pioglitazone not be used in patients with active bladder cancer and that caution be used in patients with a history of bladder cancer.

Thiazolidinediones have a number of other effects throughout the body, which are beyond the scope of this discussion. These drugs may someday have a place in the treatment of nonalcoholic fatty liver disease because they decrease hepatic fat accumulation.

Pioglitazone is marketed in tablets that contain 15 mg, 30 mg, and 45 mg of the agent. The usual starting dose is 15–30 mg once daily with a maximum recommended dose of 45 mg once daily.

Incretin-Based Therapy. Incretin hormones are synthesized in the GI tract. The major incretins are glucagon-like peptide-1 and glucose-dependent insulinotropic polypeptide. Treatment based on the incretin system includes glucagon-like peptide-1 analogs and inhibitors of dipeptidyl peptidase 4, an enzyme that breaks down glucagon-like peptide-1.

Glucagon-like peptide-1 is a peptide produced and secreted in the small intestine in response to oral nutrients. It enhances glucose stimulated insulin release from the pancreas. Other effects include decreasing appetite, suppressing glucagon, slowing gastric emptying, and weight loss. Because glucagon-like peptide-1 is broken down rapidly by dipeptidyl peptidase 4, it must be administered by continuous intravenous (IV) infusion to exert an effect. For this reason, glucagon-like peptide-1 analogs with longer half-lives have been developed; all must be given as subcutaneous injections.

Exenatide is a synthetic form of exendin-4, which is homologous to glucagon-like peptide-1. It increases insulin levels within 10 minutes of injection and is injected twice daily. Trials of exenatide have demonstrated similar efficacy to insulin in patients with type 2 diabetes mellitus who were concomitantly treated with other oral agents. Also, it can be used as a single agent in the treatment of type 2 diabetes mellitus. It is not approved for use in the treatment of type 1 diabetes mellitus. The most common adverse effect is nausea; it is generally not severe and diminishes with time. Although renal failure and pancreatitis have been reported, it is not clear whether these problems were caused by the drug or the underlying condition (45, 46). Nevertheless, clinicians are urged to consider pancreatitis when severe abdominal pain is present and to discontinue the drug when pancreatitis occurs. The drug should not be prescribed in patients with significant renal impairment. Exenatide is supplied in pens that contain either 1.2 mL or 2.4 mL of the agent. The small pen dispenses 5-microgram doses and the large pen dispenses 10-microgram doses. The usual starting dosage is 5 micrograms twice daily injected subcutaneously within 60 minutes before meals. After 1 month, the dosage can be increased to 10 micrograms twice daily if needed.

Liraglutide is a long-acting glucagon-like peptide-1 analog that can be injected once daily. Although an association between liraglutide use and thyroid cancer in rats has been demonstrated (47), the differences between rat and human thyroid physiology and the lack of abnormally elevated calcitonin levels in humans who took the drug led the FDA to approve the use of this glucagon-like peptide-1 analog for the treatment of type 2 diabetes, although not as a first-line treatment. The FDA issued a box warning about the relationship with thyroid cancer and recommends that patients be counseled about risks and symptoms of thyroid tumors. Also, it is recommended that the drug not be used in patients with a family history of medullary thyroid cancer or with multiple endocrine neoplasia type 2. Liraglutide is supplied in the form of prefilled pens that dispense doses of 0.6 mg, 1.2 mg, and 1.8 mg of the agent. The usual starting dosage is 0.6 mg injected subcutaneously once a day without regard to meals. After 1 week, if the drug is well tolerated, the dosage can be increased to 1.2 mg/d. The maximum dosage is 1.8 mg/d.

An even longer acting glucagon-like peptide-1 analog, exenatide, long-acting release, once-per-week injection, was approved by the FDA in 2012. It is injected subcutaneously at a fixed dose of 2 mg.

As noted earlier, dipeptidyl peptidase 4 is the enzyme responsible for the short half-life of glucagon-like peptide-1. Dipeptidyl peptidase 4 is present throughout the body and degrades many bioactive peptides. A number of inhibitors of dipeptidyl peptidase 4 have been developed; all are active when taken orally. Sitagliptin, saxagliptin, and linagliptin are available in the United States. Efficacy seems to be similar among these, and each can be used as single-drug therapy in type 2 diabetes mellitus or added to another agent, most often metformin. Although adverse effects are reported to be relatively minimal, these agents have been available for a relatively short time, and it is possible that other issues will arise, especially because dipeptidyl peptidase 4 is so ubiquitous.

Sitagliptin is marketed in the form of 25-mg, 50-mg, and 100-mg tablets. The usual dosage is 100 mg/d. The low-dose tablets are used for patients with moderate renal impairment (50-mg tablets) and severe renal impairment (25-mg tablets). Saxagliptin is marketed in 2.5-mg and 5-mg tablets. The usual dosage is 5 mg/d

with the 2.5-mg dose used in patients with moderate or severe
renal impairment or those taking certain drugs that interact with
cytochrome P450. Linagliptin is marketed in the form of 5-mg
tablets, and the usual dosage is 5 mg/d. Because the latter drug
is eliminated in the enterohepatic circulation and only 5% is
excreted in the urine, no dosage adjustment is needed in patients
with renal impairment.

Alpha-glucosidase inhibitors are orally active agents that
inhibit the action of GI alpha-glucosidases, thereby slowing the
breakdown of polysaccharides to monosaccharides, slowing the
absorption of glucose, and decreasing postprandial circulating
glucose levels. The two agents available in the United States,
acarbose and miglitol, have been primarily used in the treatment
of type 2 diabetes mellitus and are effective, although perhaps
less so than other agents (48). The main adverse effect of these
drugs is flatulence, sometimes accompanied by diarrhea. This
is highly prevalent and may limit their acceptance. Often, it is
helpful to start therapy at a low dose and increase gradually.
Although most acarbose remains in the GI tract and very little is
absorbed, hepatitis has been reported in patients taking acarbose,
albeit rarely (47). The hepatitis generally improved when the drug
was discontinued. Miglitol is systemically absorbed and cleared
by the kidneys.

Acarbose is supplied as 25-mg, 50-mg, and-100 mg tablets.
The usual starting dosage is 25 mg three times a day with the
first bite of each meal. Patients who experience GI adverse effects
with the three-times-a-day dosage may start with a once-per-day
dosage and slowly increase to three times per day. Dosage may
then be titrated at 3–4-week intervals based on postprandial glucose levels. Maximum recommended dosage is 50 mg three times
a day for individuals who weigh 60 kg (132 lb) or less and 100 mg
three times a day for those who weigh more than 60 kg (132 lb).
Miglitol is supplied as 25-mg, 50-mg, and 1,200-mg tablets, and
the dosage is similar to that of acarbose.

Amylin is a peptide produced and stored in pancreatic β-cells
and secreted at the same time as insulin. Amylin slows gastric
emptying, inhibits glucagon release, and decreases appetite.
Pramlintide is an analog of amylin that is injected subcutaneously

at mealtime. It is approved only for use in patients who are already taking insulin and in whom control is not optimal with insulin alone. This drug has been demonstrated, in randomized trials, to reduce HbA_{1c} levels modestly (average, 0.6–0.7%) in patients with type 1 diabetes mellitus and type 2 diabetes mellitus when combined with insulin therapy. It does not ordinarily cause hypoglycemia, although delay of gastric emptying may result in hypoglycemia in patients who take rapidly acting insulin analogs. Adverse effects include nausea, most noticeable in the first month of treatment. Pramlintide is injected immediately before meals and must be given at a site different from that of insulin injection. When this drug is introduced, it may be necessary to reduce the preprandial insulin dosage by 25–50% at first. The usual starting dose for patients with type 1 diabetes mellitus is 15 micrograms before each meal, increased by 15 micrograms every 3–7 days until a dose of 60 micrograms is reached. For individuals with type 2 diabetes mellitus who take basal insulin, the starting dose is 60 micrograms, increased to 120 micrograms with each meal, if tolerated.

CASE NO. 2. A 30-year-old woman, gravida 2, para 2 was successfully treated with diet for GDM in her previous pregnancy, which was 2 years ago. She did not follow advice to have a follow-up OGTT at the time of her postpartum visit. She comes in because she has symptoms of vaginitis, and monilia is diagnosed. An HbA_{1c} test is ordered; the result is 8% (estimated average glucose level, 183 mg/dL).

This patient has type 2 diabetes mellitus. She should be counseled as described in Box 3. A thorough medical history should be obtained with particular attention to the presence or absence of CV risk factors. A thorough examination should be performed, starting with measurement of blood pressure, determination of weight and height, and calculation of BMI. Her feet should be examined for signs of neuropathy and vascular disease. This patient should be referred for a periodontal examination and a dilated retinal evaluation. A fasting lipid profile and urinary albumin excretion measurement should be obtained and she should be referred for nutritional consultation and diabetes self-management education, including recommendations for physical activity at least 150 minutes per week. She will be instructed regarding self-glucose monitoring, which should be performed before meals; her goal should be to achieve a value of 70–130 mg/dL. If her glucose values are not normalized within a few months by lifestyle modification, she should start taking metformin, 500 mg at breakfast, with titration of the dose as described earlier. Vaginitis also should be treated; it will be less likely to recur once the diabetes is well controlled. Because she would like to have another child, she should be counseled regarding the need for family planning until such time as her HbA_{1c} value is less than 7%. Although barrier methods might be reasonable if the patient is highly motivated and likely to decrease her HbA_{1c} value rapidly, more reliable methods, such as an intrauterine device or a progestin insert would be preferable. A preconception visit should be scheduled after allowing a reasonable time for her to become accustomed to the diagnosis of diabetes mellitus.

Prevention of Complications

OBESITY

Patients with type 2 diabetes mellitus who are obese can reduce the likelihood of long-term complications by losing weight. The primary approach is developing and maintaining a healthy lifestyle as outlined in the section "Prevention." However, for many individuals this strategy is not successful. For individuals with type 2 diabetes mellitus whose BMI is 35 or more, particularly those whose glucose is not controlled with the recommended pharmacologic and lifestyle interventions, bariatric surgery has been demonstrated to result in normalization of glucose control in 78% of cases (49). Procedures also may help patients whose BMI is more than 40 and who do not have diabetes mellitus or other complications. A number of different procedures are available. The adjustable gastric banding and the Roux-en-Y gastric bypass are the most frequently performed procedures. The adjustable gastric band constricts the esophageal–gastric junction, can be placed laparoscopically in many patients, and works by restricting food intake. In 2011, the FDA approved the adjustable gastric band for individuals with diabetes and a BMI of more than 30. The Roux-en-Y procedure is performed either laparoscopically or as open surgery and involves bypassing most of the stomach, duodenum, and upper part of the small intestine. Because much absorption of food occurs in the bypassed region, food absorption and intake are decreased. Randomized trials have demonstrated superiority of Roux-en-Y, biliopancreatic diversion, or sleeve gastrectomy procedures over medical therapy in reversing diabetes mellitus (50). The improvement in glucose metabolism appears to predate the major weight loss, which suggests that weight loss may not be the only important factor. Bariatric surgery has a number of potential risks and complications and should be undertaken in the setting of a team that can carry out lifelong support and medical monitoring.

CARDIOVASCULAR DISEASE

Cardiovascular disease is the leading cause of death and morbidity in individuals with diabetes. Although normalization of glycemia is important in preventing CV complications, control of blood pressure and dyslipidemia also can lower the risk of CV events. The ADA and the American Heart Association have jointly published recommendations for the prevention of CV disease in individuals with diabetes mellitus (51). These recommendations include weight control and medical nutrition therapy to limit intake of trans unsaturated fatty acids and sodium and to reduce low-density lipoprotein cholesterol levels. Regular physical activity is emphasized. Blood pressure monitoring and control are essential. The goal should be to achieve less than 130 mm Hg systolic blood pressure and less than 80 mm Hg diastolic blood pressure. Hypertension should be treated with an angiotensin-converting enzyme (ACE) inhibitor or angiotensin receptor blocker, and renal function should be evaluated at regular intervals. Annual lipid measurement is recommended. Statin therapy is recommended based on risk factors (51).

NEPHROPATHY

Diabetic nephropathy, also termed "diabetic kidney disease," is the leading cause of end-stage renal disease in the United States and accounts for 45% of all cases of renal disease. Diabetic nephropathy occurs in approximately one third of patients with diabetes mellitus. Although at one time it was seen primarily in individuals with type 1 diabetes mellitus, the ongoing epidemics of obesity and type 2 diabetes mellitus have reversed this trend. Diabetic nephropathy progresses over time. The earliest changes, which are generally clinically undetectable, are associated with hyperperfusion of the kidneys and hyperfunction in which the glomerular filtration rate (GFR) is increased. The earliest recognizable sign is microalbuminuria, defined as 30–299 micrograms of albumin per milligram of creatinine on a spot urine test, which should be present in at least two of three samples over 3–6 months. This may progress to macroalbuminuria, 300 micrograms or more of albumin per milligram of creatinine. Although microalbuminuria does not always progress, macroalbuminuria generally progresses over time, culminating in end-stage renal disease. The ADA recommends an annual test to assess albumin excretion in patients with type 1 diabetes mellitus with duration of 5 years or greater. In patients with type 2 diabetes mellitus, an annual test is recommended from the time of diagnosis, presumably because many cases of type 2 diabetes mellitus are not diagnosed for many years after the onset. The recommended method for albuminuria screening is obtaining the spot urine albumin to creatinine ratio. A 24-hour urine test or timed urine collection also can be used but are more complicated for the patient. All adults with diabetes mellitus should have a serum creatinine measurement annually because reduced renal function can sometimes be present even without albuminuria. The creatinine level can be used to calculate a GFR using a GFR calculator, such as that found online at http://www.nkdep.nih.gov/lab-evaluation/gfr-calculators.shtml. Although normal rates vary by age because GFR decreases over time, values of more than 90 mL/min are considered normal, 60–89 mL/min mildly impaired, and less than 60 mL/min moderately decreased. The ADA recommends referral to a nephrologist when GFR is less than 30 mL/min or when the cause of kidney disease is uncertain (26).

Treatment of type 1 diabetes mellitus and of type 2 diabetes mellitus aimed at near euglycemia has been demonstrated to delay the onset of microalbuminuria and macroalbuminuria in randomized trials and to delay progression of nephropathy (31, 32). The ADA recommends that ACE inhibitors or angiotensin receptor blockers be used in patients with diabetes mellitus and microalbuminuria or macroalbuminuria (26). If hypertension is present and is not controlled with these drugs, then additional therapy should be used (eg, calcium channel blockers, β-blockers, and diuretics). Restriction of dietary protein intake may help slow progression, particularly when nephropathy is progressing despite the aforementioned interventions.

RETINOPATHY

Diabetes mellitus is the leading cause of blindness among American adults, causing more than 10,000 individuals to lose their vision annually (52). Retinopathy may begin to develop as early as 4–7 years before the diagnosis of type 2 diabetes mellitus, whereas most often it is not present in patients with type 1 diabetes mellitus until at least 5 years after the diagnosis. This is ascribed to the slow and silent onset of type 2 diabetes mellitus compared with the usual sudden onset of type 1 diabetes mellitus. Retinopathy is the result of injury to retinal arterioles and capillary endothelial cells. Background retinopathy includes microaneurysms, exudates, and hemorrhages of progressing severity. Proliferative retinopathy involves new vessel formation, termed "neovascularization." These new vessels are fragile and bleed easily, which leads to hemorrhage into the vitreous that can cause transient loss of vision. The subsequent scarring can cause retinal detachment and permanent loss of vision. Another mechanism of vision loss is macular edema. The presence and severity of retinopathy correlates with the duration of diabetes mellitus. A number of pathophysiologic mechanisms have been postulated to contribute to the development of retinopathy, all of which are associated with hyperglycemia. Other contributing risk factors include hypertension and nephropathy. In addition to retinopathy, vision loss caused by cataracts and glaucoma is more prevalent in individuals with diabetes.

Randomized trials have shown that intensive metabolic control can reduce the likelihood of retinopathy or its progression in patients with type 1 diabetes mellitus (53) and type 2 diabetes mellitus (32, 54). In the latter study, treatment of dyslipidemia

also was found to have a significant beneficial effect in preventing the progression of retinopathy, although blood pressure
control was not independently effective. The ADA recommends
optimization of glycemic control and blood pressure control to
decrease or slow the progression of retinopathy (26). For type 1
diabetes mellitus, a dilated eye examination by an ophthalmologist or optometrist should be performed within 5 years of onset
of diabetes. For type 2 diabetes mellitus, because of the typical lag
between onset and diagnosis, the initial eye examination should
be performed shortly after the diagnosis is established. Annual
examinations are recommended thereafter. Once changes, such
as macular edema, severe background (nonproliferative) retinopathy, or proliferative retinopathy have occurred, consideration of
laser photocoagulation is recommended to reduce the risk of
vision loss. The ADA also notes that retinopathy is not a contrain-
dication to aspirin therapy for cardioprotection because the risk of
retinal hemorrhage is not increased by the use of aspirin.

NEUROPATHY

Diabetic neuropathy comprises a range of disorders, all of which
are caused by damage to nerve fibers that results from diabetes
mellitus (55). These syndromes are present in approximately 10%
of patients at the time of diagnosis of diabetes, and more than 50%
of diabetic patients will develop neuropathy over the long term
(56). The various neuropathies generally are classified as either
diffuse or focal. Diffuse neuropathies are subclassified into distal
symmetrical sensorimotor polyneuropathy and diabetic autonomic
neuropathy. The diffuse neuropathies are the most common.

Distal symmetrical sensorimotor polyneuropathy starts periph-
erally, and sensory deficits predominate in the early stages. The
longest nerve fibers are affected first, such that the feet and
hands lose sensation. Proprioception and light touch are lost
when large nerve fibers are affected, whereas pain and temperature perception are impaired with small fiber disease. Typical
symptoms include paresthesias, neuropathic pain, and hyper-
esthesias. In early disease, deep tendon reflexes may be diminished or lost, with the Achilles tendon typically affected. The
changes may progress to the hands as well. Motor changes may
follow, with weakness of foot muscles and increased pressure

on the metatarsal heads. Plantar calluses may progress to pressure ulcers and infection. This may ultimately lead to amputation, with diabetes being the most common cause of amputations in the United States (1).

Diabetic autonomic neuropathy, often present with distal symmetrical sensorimotor polyneuropathy, may impair any sympathetic or parasympathetic function. Common manifestations include gastroparesis, erectile dysfunction, female sexual dysfunction, neurogenic bladder, orthostatic hypotension, resting tachycardia, dry skin or excessive sweating, and diarrhea or constipation.

Focal neuropathies are less common and may affect a single peripheral or cranial nerve (mononeuropathy), nerve roots (radiculopathy), or plexus of nerves (plexopathy). Neuropathies of the median and ulnar nerve are the most common mononeuropathies. Mononeuropathy generally is believed to be caused by vasculopathy of the blood supply of the particular nerve.

Establishment of excellent blood glucose control has been shown to prevent or delay diabetic neuropathy in randomized trials of patients with type 1 diabetes mellitus (57). Although not as well documented, it is likely that good diabetic control also can prevent or delay neuropathy in patients with type 2 diabetes mellitus (55). The ADA recommends that all patients with diabetes be screened for distal symmetrical sensorimotor polyneuropathy at the time of diagnosis, and screened for diabetic autonomic neuropathy at diagnosis of type 2 diabetes mellitus and 5 years after the diagnosis of type 1 diabetes mellitus (26). Simple clinical tests should be repeated at least annually thereafter. Recommended screening tests for distal symmetrical sensorimotor polyneuropathy include testing for pinprick sensation, vibration perception, and 10-g monofilament pressure sensation at the distal plantar aspects of the great toes and metatarsal joints. Loss of vibration perception or monofilament sensation is predictive of diabetic foot ulcers. Recommended screening for diabetic autonomic neuropathy includes inquiring about exercise intolerance, constipation, symptoms of gastroparesis, erectile dysfunction, and hypoglycemia unawareness. Signs include resting tachycardia and orthostatic hypotension. Symptomatic treatment is available for many of these problems, but good glucose control is of critical importance.

FOOT CARE

Both diabetic neuropathy and peripheral arterial disease may lead to ulceration and ultimately amputation of limbs, particularly the feet. Amputations are among the leading causes of disability in individuals with diabetes. The ADA recommends an annual comprehensive foot examination for all individuals with diabetes mellitus (26). Components of the examination are listed in Box 5. Patients with neuropathy or evidence of increased plantar pressure should be fitted for walking shoes or athletic shoes that cushion the feet and redistribute pressure. Foot care specialists

---

Box 5. Components of Annual Comprehensive Foot Examination to Identify Risk Factors for Ulcers and Amputations

- Inspection
- Assessment of foot pulses
- Testing for loss of protective sensation (10-g monofilament)
- One of the following tests:
    - —Tuning fork (128-Hz) test for vibration perception
    - —Test for pinprick sensation
    - —Test for ankle reflexes
- General foot self-care education
- Multidisciplinary approach for those with high risk*, foot ulcers, or a previous amputation
- Referral to a foot care specialist for lifelong surveillance and preventive care in the following situations:
    - —Loss of protective sensation
    - —Structural abnormalities
    - —A history of prior lower extremity complications
    - —The patient is a smoker

(continued)

> ## Box 5. Components of Annual Comprehensive Foot Examination to Identify Risk Factors for Ulcers and Amputations *(continued)*
>
> - Screening for peripheral arterial disease by obtaining history of claudication and assessing pedal pulses. Consider obtaining ankle brachial index[†] because peripheral arterial disease often is asymptomatic.
>
> *The risk of ulcers and amputation is increased in individuals who have the following risk factors:
> - Previous amputation
> - Past foot ulcer history
> - Peripheral neuropathy
> - Foot deformity
> - Peripheral vascular disease
> - Visual impairment
> - Diabetic nephropathy (especially patients receiving dialysis)
> - Poor glycemic control
> - Cigarette smoking
>
> [†]Ankle brachial index is the ratio of systolic blood pressure in the posterior tibial and dorsalis pedis arteries (measured with a Doppler device) and the brachial systolic blood pressure. An ankle brachial index greater than 0.9 suggests normal peripheral arteries.
>
> Data from Standards of medical care in diabetes--2012. American Diabetes Association. Diabetes Care 2012;35 Suppl 1:S11–63 *and* Boulton AJ, Armstrong DG, Albert SF, Frykberg RG, Hellman R, Kirkman MS, et al. Comprehensive foot examination and risk assessment: a report of the task force of the foot care interest group of the American Diabetes Association, with endorsement by the American Association of Clinical Endocrinologists. American Diabetes Association. American Association of Clinical Endocrinologists. Diabetes Care 2008;31:1679–85.

can débride calluses and may prescribe custom-molded shoes for specific deformities. Referral to a podiatrist, orthopedic surgeon, or vascular surgeon may be necessary for management of foot ulcers and wound care.

DIABETIC KETOACIDOSIS

Diabetic ketoacidosis, which consists of hyperglycemia and elevated levels of ketone acids in the bloodstream, is a medical emergency. It is not caused by overabundance of glucose but rather by relative or absolute lack of insulin. The lack of insulin leads to breakdown of triglycerides in adipose tissue to liberate free fatty acids, which are then transported to the liver where they are degraded to ketone bodies. The lack of insulin also causes increased hepatic gluconeogenesis and glycogenolysis, elevating circulating glucose levels. Patients with diabetic ketoacidosis manifest symptoms, such as Kussmaul respiration (deep breathing), nausea and vomiting, abdominal pain, and mental aberrations. Signs may include a fruity odor on the breath, tachycardia, and hypotension. Laboratory testing reveals low pH, low serum bicarbonate level, and increasing anion gap. Treatment of diabetic ketoacidosis should be provided by a physician with expertise in managing this condition. Patients with diabetic ketoacidosis are dehydrated because of the osmotic diuretic effect of hyperglycemia; serum osmolality increases as a result. Fluid volume deficits typically are in the range of 3–6 liters. When dehydration is severe, renal plasma flow decreases, which leads to further hyperglycemia because of the inability to dispose of glucose in the urine. Therefore, the first component of therapy is IV fluid replacement, typically normal saline solution, 1 L/hr over the first 2 hours, then 0.5 L/hr. Regular insulin is given intravenously, typically in a bolus of 20 units, then 5–10 units per hour. Once the circulating glucose level decreases below 200–250 mg/dL, 5% dextrose should be added, and the rate of insulin infusion may be reduced. Serum potassium levels may be normal or elevated, but typically, total body potassium is deficient. As IV insulin drives glucose into cells, potassium levels decrease, and potassium supplementation is necessary.

HYPEROSMOLAR NONKETOTIC STATE

Patients with type 2 diabetes mellitus produce insulin, generally in sufficient amounts to avoid ketoacidosis. Consequently, when their condition is out of control and they become dehydrated because of the osmotic effect of hyperglycemia, their glucose levels increase because of the decreased renal plasma flow. They become hyperosmolar, and this may lead to confusion and then coma. As in ketoacidosis, the most important first step is IV fluid administration to reverse the dehydration and insulin administration to decrease glucose levels. Electrolyte levels generally need to be corrected. In addition, attention must be paid to correction of the underlying cause of dehydration.

Reproductive Concerns

Family Planning

Reliable and safe contraception is a critical component of planning for diabetic pregnancy. Because of the importance of establishing excellent metabolic control before conception, every pregnancy of a woman with diabetes mellitus should be planned.
A wide range of family planning options are available. Low-dose combination oral contraceptives are a reasonable choice for women with diabetes mellitus who are younger than 35 years, do not have vascular disease, and do not smoke. For women with vascular disease, progestin-only formulations may be used. Injections of long-acting depot medroxyprogesterone acetate (DMPA) may worsen insulin resistance and increase the likelihood of developing type 2 diabetes mellitus in Latino and Navajo women (groups with a high prevalence of type 2 diabetes mellitus) with previous GDM, although available data are reassuring regarding effects in patients with established diabetes mellitus (58). Progestin-containing and copper-containing intrauterine devices may be used by women with diabetes mellitus and have the advantage of lasting 5 years or 10 years, respectively, without the need to remember to take a medication daily. Long-lasting progesterone implants similarly are reasonable for women with diabetes mellitus to use. Barrier methods have no effect on diabetes mellitus but are somewhat less effective and require administration with each coital episode. Permanent sterilization is an appropriate option for a woman with diabetes mellitus whose family is complete or who has significant vascular disease.

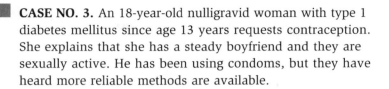

CASE NO. 3. An 18-year-old nulligravid woman with type 1 diabetes mellitus since age 13 years requests contraception. She explains that she has a steady boyfriend and they are sexually active. He has been using condoms, but they have heard more reliable methods are available.

This is an excellent opportunity to counsel this patient about diabetes mellitus and pregnancy. Although she seeks contraception, this visit also should serve as a preconception visit. It should be ascertained whether she is receiving appropriate diabetes care from her primary care physician and whether she shows any evidence of diabetic vasculopathy because this may influence the choice of contraception. If she is a smoker, this visit also is a potential teachable moment regarding smoking cessation. It is an opportunity to point out the additional risk from smoking for combination oral contraceptive users, for pregnancy, and for her overall health and the health of those who inhabit the same environment with her. Because she is already sexually active, her decision to seek effective contraception and the potential consequences of an unintended pregnancy for women in general and those with diabetes mellitus in particular should be reinforced. Her most recent HbA_{1c} test result should be recorded and she should be counseled that when and if pregnancy may be desired, it will be important to make sure that her HbA_{1c} level is below 7% to reduce the risk of congenital malformations in the offspring. Although Pap test screening is not recommended until age 21 years, the patient should be counseled and tested for sexually transmitted infections and should be counseled regarding safe sex. These measures may be performed without cervical cytology and, in the asymptomatic patient, without the introduction of a speculum. Because this patient indicates she is not a smoker, she may choose any of the short-acting or long-acting forms of reversible contraception.

Infertility

Although no apparent increased likelihood of infertility exists in women with type 1 diabetes mellitus, those with type 2 diabetes mellitus who have PCOS often experience anovulation and may need intervention to become pregnant. Metformin, an insulin sensitizer, often is used to treat patients with metabolic syndrome. Its use may be associated with reversal of the anovulatory state, so that many previously infertile women conceive after starting this medication. Two randomized, blinded trials in infertile women with PCOS demonstrated that metformin was more effective in achieving pregnancy compared with ovarian diathermy (which reduces the estrogen-producing mass in the ovaries and may trigger ovulation [59]) and compared with clomiphene citrate (60). Pregnancies conceived while participants were taking metformin also were less likely to end in spontaneous abortion than with either of the other two interventions. The metformin was discontinued as soon as pregnancy was diagnosed with sensitive hCG assays. When the NIH-sponsored Cooperative Multicenter Reproductive Medicine Network performed a large (N = 626) randomized, double-blind trial of metformin versus clomiphene citrate versus both drugs, clomiphene was superior to metformin in conception rate and live birth rate, and no significant difference in the spontaneous abortion rate was noted, although the trend was higher in patients who received metformin (21%) than in those who received clomiphene citrate (8%) (61). Multiple births were more frequent with clomiphene citrate. It remains somewhat controversial whether metformin reduces the spontaneous abortion rate in patients with PCOS who conceive, but if metformin is effective, it needs to be administered only around the time of conception because the apparent beneficial effect is present even when the drug is discontinued as soon as pregnancy can be diagnosed. Metformin also has been suggested for treatment of patients with PCOS throughout pregnancy because of postulated benefits, such as reducing the likelihood of GDM, preeclampsia, and preterm birth. A review of available data, including a large randomized trial, concluded that metformin does not have such benefits and no reason exists to prescribe it for these indications (62). Because metformin has been demonstrated to cross the placenta from mother to fetus, with higher levels in the fetal than maternal compartments (63), the theoretical potential exists for unknown fetal effects.

Effects During Pregnancy

A number of risks are associated with pregnancy in women with preexisting diabetes mellitus. Gestational diabetes mellitus, which is abnormal glucose metabolism with onset or first diagnosis during pregnancy, carries risks of a similar nature, albeit generally less severe. These risks will be discussed in a subsequent section. Women with preexisting diabetes mellitus are prone to problems that involve themselves and their developing fetuses. Most, if not all, of these potential problems are associated with elevated circulating glucose levels. The altered hormonal milieu of pregnancy, with resulting insulin resistance, is primarily responsible. Management focuses on attaining and maintaining glucose control as close to euglycemia as is practical before conception and throughout the pregnancy.

MATERNAL EFFECTS

Diabetic vasculopathy may be affected by pregnancy. Pregnancy appears to have an independent adverse effect on retinopathy, although the need for rapid institution of tight metabolic control to prevent congenital malformations and other problems also may contribute to the progression of retinopathy. The level of proteinuria in patients with diabetic nephropathy typically increases as pregnancy progresses, at least partially because of increased renal plasma flow, but it is uncertain whether pregnancy exerts an independent permanent effect on the progression of diabetic kidney disease (64). Myocardial infarction caused by coronary artery disease is relatively rare during or shortly after pregnancy, occurring in 1 of 36,000 deliveries in a California database; however, it was four times more common in women with diabetes than in the general population (65). Although gastroparesis may worsen, other potential effects of pregnancy on diabetic neuropathy, if any, are not well defined.

A number of pregnancy complications are more likely in diabetic pregnancy. Preeclampsia and other hypertensive disorders are more common in pregnant women with diabetes, particularly when vascular disease, such as nephropathy, chronic hypertension, or proliferative retinopathy, is present. Diabetic ketoacidosis, caused by insulin deficiency in individuals with type 1 diabetes mellitus, appears to be more frequent. Diabetic ketoacidosis also may occur in pregnant women with type 2 diabetes mellitus under conditions of metabolic stress. This is a particularly worrisome complication because fetal death may result.

FETAL AND NEONATAL EFFECTS

Fetal malformations occur three to four times more frequently in diabetic pregnancies relative to the 2–3% malformation rate in those of the general population (66). Hyperglycemia during the first 8–10 weeks, the period of organogenesis, appears to be responsible as evidenced by the direct relationship between elevated maternal HbA_{1c} levels and the likelihood of anomalies in the offspring (67). A number of observational studies have demonstrated that first-trimester HbA_{1c} levels in the range of 10% are associated with a risk of anomalies of 20% or more (68), whereas levels within 3% of the upper limit of normal (less than 6.3%) are compatible with the risk similar to that seen in the general population.

By the end of the first trimester, the fetal pancreas is capable of producing and releasing insulin in response to elevated glucose levels, and fetal hyperinsulinemia assumes the primary role in causing adverse outcomes. Fetal hyperinsulinemia can lead to fetal overgrowth that results in macrosomia, difficult delivery with an increased likelihood of cesarean delivery, and an increased possibility of shoulder dystocia with potential brachial plexus injury. Intrauterine growth restriction (IUGR) is increased in the presence of diabetic vasculopathy, especially when hypertension is present. Premature birth, either spontaneous or medically indicated, is more common in diabetic pregnancies. Prematurely born infants of diabetic women are more likely than other infants to have complications of prematurity at a given gestational age. Respiratory distress syndrome is particularly a problem when premature birth complicates poorly controlled diabetes. Neonatal cardiac hypertrophy, plethora, hyperbilirubinemia, hypocalcemia, and hypoglycemia are all more frequent in infants of diabetic women than in other infants. Stillbirth also is more frequent in diabetic pregnancies in which glucose control is suboptimal, particularly as term approaches.

Preconception Care

The most critical component of preconception care of the woman with diabetes is counseling; the patient should be informed that an elevated glucose level before pregnancy and during organogenesis is associated with an increased likelihood of congenital malformations. The ADA recommends that the HbA$_{1c}$ level be as close to normal as possible, with a goal of less than 7% (corresponding to an estimated average glucose level of 155 mg/dL), before conception (26). Therefore, every visit to a health care provider by a woman with the potential to bear children should be considered a preconception visit. Self-management knowledge and skills should be assessed and reinforced to enable the patient to be successful in achieving the glycemia goals. If the woman does not desire pregnancy soon, she should be offered safe and effective contraception until pregnancy is intended. An initial preconception care visit should include assessment of glycemic control by review of glucose self-monitoring logs and measurement of HbA$_{1c}$ levels (64). Components of the medical history, physical examination, and laboratory testing are similar to those described for the initial evaluation of nonpregnant patients with diabetes mellitus. Referral for dilated retinal examination by an ophthalmologist, measurement of urinary protein excretion, assessment of presence or absence of neuropathy, and CV disease screening are particularly pertinent. If the patient's HbA$_{1c}$ level is not in the target range, a treatment plan should be agreed upon and conception should be delayed until glycemia goals are met so that the risk of congenital malformation is as low as possible. Patients with proliferative retinopathy should be referred for treatment by an ophthalmologist; laser therapy is safe and effective during pregnancy, but ideally is performed before pregnancy. Patients with nephropathy should be referred to a nephrologist so that a therapeutic relationship can be established to facilitate long-term management of this chronic condition.

Patents with insulin-treated diabetes mellitus should work with the health care team to adjust the insulin dosage to achieve target levels of glycemic control. When problems, such as hypoglycemia unawareness, are present, it may be necessary to adjust targets upward to avoid serious complications. The use of oral antidiabetic agents during pregnancy is controversial. At one time, glyburide was believed not to cross the placenta, but subsequent pharmacokinetic studies demonstrated cord blood levels that averaged 70% of simultaneous maternal levels (69). Although the absolute levels were quite low in cord blood, they were similarly low in maternal blood; fetal levels at times when maternal levels are in the therapeutic range were not determined. Metformin, another antidiabetic drug that is widely used, crosses the placenta readily and fetal levels may exceed maternal levels (63). Even less is known about potential fetal effects of other antidiabetic medications. Although it is possible that metformin or glyburide or both may be beneficial to the fetus and neither drug has been shown to cause harm, essential studies of animal models are lacking, as are long-term studies of human offspring exposed in utero. As the understanding of in utero metabolic programming expands, it would seem most appropriate, if possible, to avoid using these oral agents during pregnancy to avoid exposure of the fetus with unknown consequences. The American College of Obstetricians and Gynecologists (the College) recommends that the use of oral agents during pregnancy should be limited and individualized until data regarding safety and efficacy become available (68). The ADA recommends the discontinuation of oral agents, and patients with type 2 diabetes mellitus who need pharmacologic treatment should switch to insulin before conception (64). When metformin or glyburide is prescribed for a pregnant woman, she should be informed of the fact that the drug crosses the placenta and reaches the fetus; although no adverse short-term effects have been demonstrated, potential long-term effects are unknown.

One of the most important components of preconception care is the introduction of the critical concept of a health care team. With the patient at its center, core members of the team include a physician or physicians experienced in the care of diabetes and pregnancy, diabetes nurse educator, dietitian, and social worker. Other members of the team, as appropriate, may include an ophthalmologist, dentist, nephrologist, podiatrist, and pediatrician or neonatologist.

The patient's medication history should be reviewed. Many medications typically taken by individuals with diabetes mellitus are relatively or absolutely contraindicated during pregnancy.

For example, ACE inhibitors and angiotensin receptor blockers generally are prescribed for their renoprotective effects. However, ACE inhibitors taken in the first trimester have been associated with an increased risk of congenital malformations, cardiac in particular (70). Data regarding angiotensin receptor blockers in the first trimester are not available, but it would be prudent to discontinue these drugs before conception, if possible. Furthermore, second- and third-trimester use of ACE inhibitors and angiotensin receptor blockers has been associated with oligohydramnios and impaired renal function in the fetus and neonate with possible renal failure after birth. Therefore, these drugs should be avoided during pregnancy. Patients who take these drugs for hypertension should be prescribed other classes of medications, such as β-blockers, calcium channel blockers, or methyldopa. Statins also are considered to be contraindicated during pregnancy because of concerns about teratogenicity although a clear association has not been established. These drugs should be discontinued before conception.

During the period when metabolic control is being optimized, the patient should be advised to use an effective and reversible form of contraception, with the understanding that this will be discontinued once the diabetic control goals are met.

After the initial preconception visit, close follow-up should be maintained to encourage achievement of therapeutic goals. Visits with the health care team should be arranged every 1–2 months and interspersed with frequent telephone or e-mail contact to monitor progress and adjust the treatment regimen. Once the patient's HbA_{1c} level has reached the target of less than 7% (or a higher target, if necessary, based on the clinician's judgment of what level of control is practical for this patient without causing frequent hypoglycemia), the patient is advised to discontinue contraception and is, in essence, "cleared for pregnancy."

Preexisting Diabetes Mellitus

All pregnant women become increasingly insulin resistant secondary to placental hormones. Most pregnant women are able to augment their insulin production to maintain a state of euglycemia. Some are unable to do so and develop GDM, which will be discussed in a subsequent section of this monograph. Women with preexisting type 1 diabetes mellitus and type 2 diabetes mellitus experience the same increase in insulin resistance as do other pregnant women. Although, in the past, more pregnant women had type 1 diabetes mellitus than type 2 diabetes mellitus, in recent years, the proportion of pregnant women with type 2 diabetes mellitus has increased, similar to the trend for type 2 diabetes mellitus in young adults throughout the United States (71). Nationwide hospital discharge data reveal that the women with type 1 diabetes mellitus accounted for 2.4 per 1,000 deliveries in 1994 and 3.3 per 1,000 deliveries in 2004, a 33% increase. However, deliveries among women with type 2 diabetes mellitus increased from 0.9 per 1,000 to 4.2 per 1,000 in the same period, a 366% increase, which is more common than deliveries among women with type 1 diabetes mellitus (71). As noted earlier, patients who use oral antidiabetic agents should take insulin in anticipation of pregnancy. Should pregnancy occur without the benefit of a preconception visit, insulin should be instituted at the time of initiation of care.

The management of diabetes mellitus in pregnancy must focus on excellent glucose control achieved with the use of a careful combination of diet, exercise, and insulin therapy. Patients may need to be seen by their physicians as often as every 1–2 weeks during the first two trimesters and weekly after 28–30 weeks of gestation. Self-capillary glucose monitoring is performed at least four times daily. Goals for glucose control include a fasting glucose level of 95 mg/dL or less, prandial glucose level of 100 mg/dL or less, 1-hour postprandial glucose level of 140 mg/dL or less, or 2-hour postprandial glucose level of 120 mg/dL or less (68).

DIET

During pregnancy with a singleton fetus, daily caloric requirements are increased approximately 340 kcal above basal needs in the second trimester and 450 kcal above basal needs in the third trimester. Carbohydrate counting increases dietary flexibility and is useful as long as the total daily caloric intake is considered to avoid excessive weight gain. A registered dietitian will be of value in providing an individualized nutrition program. The Institute of Medicine issued guidelines for weight gain during pregnancy in 2009. The current recommended goals based on prepregnancy BMI are as follows (72):

- Underweight (BMI, less than 18.5): gain 28–40 lb
- Normal weight (BMI, 18.5–24.9): gain 25–35 lb
- Overweight (BMI, 25–29.9): gain 15–25 lb
- Obese (BMI, 30 or more): gain 11–20 lb

The Institute of Medicine gestational weight gain guidelines provide clinicians with a basis for practice. Clinicians who provide care for pregnant women should determine a woman's BMI at the initial prenatal visit (an online BMI calculator is available at http://www.nhlbi.nih.gov/guidelines/obesity/BMI/bmicalc.htm). It is important to discuss appropriate weight gain, diet, and exercise at the initial visit and periodically throughout the pregnancy. Individualized care and clinical judgment are necessary in the management of the overweight or obese woman who is gaining (or wishes to gain) less weight than recommended but has an appropriately growing fetus. Balancing the risks of fetal growth (in the large-for-gestational-age fetus and the small-for-gestational-age fetus), obstetric complications, and maternal weight retention is essential but will remain challenging until research provides evidence to further refine the recommendations for gestational weight gain, especially among women with high degrees of obesity (73).

Women with normal body weight (BMI, 18.5–24.9) usually require 30–35 kcal/kg/d. Women who are less than 90% of desirable body weight may need to increase their caloric requirements to 30–40 kcal/kg/d, whereas those who are more than 120% of desirable body weight should decrease their caloric intake to 24 kcal/kg/d. Caloric composition includes 40–50% from complex, high-fiber carbohydrates; 20% from protein; and 30–40% from primarily unsaturated fats. The calories may be distributed as follows: 10–20% at breakfast; 20–30% at lunch; 30–40% for dinner; and up to 30% for snacks, especially a bedtime snack to reduce nocturnal hypoglycemia. Artificial sweeteners, such as saccharin, aspartame, neotame, sucralose, and acesulfame potassium may be safely used in moderate amounts.

INSULIN

Table 5 illustrates the goals for glucose control during pregnancy as recommended by the College and the ADA. Although slight differences in emphasis exist between the two, the recommendations are overall quite similar. Frequent self-monitoring of blood glucose levels, at least four times daily, is essential. The fasting glucose level reflects the action of overnight basal insulin; this may be intermediate-acting insulin administered before dinner or at bedtime or, alternatively, long-acting insulin administered at any time of the day or night because it has no peak of action. If glucose levels are tested before meals, they should reflect the action of basal insulin as described earlier. Levels measured after meals reflect the action of recent short-acting insulin doses or earlier intermediate-acting insulin doses. Insulin doses are adjusted by 10–20% in response to values above or below targets. Adjustments in patients with type 1 diabetes mellitus generally are smaller than for those with type 2 diabetes mellitus. As mentioned previously, two sizes of insulin syringes exist, 0.5 mL and 1 mL. The usual U-100 insulin contains 100 units per milliliter. The smaller, 0.5-mL syringes are calibrated in 1-unit increments, whereas the 1-mL syringes are calibrated in 2-unit increments. Thus, when

Table 5. Goals for Capillary Glucose Control During Pregnancy

	Recommendations	
Markers	American College of Obstetricians and Gynecologists	American Diabetes Association
Fasting glucose level	Less than 95 mg/dL	60–99 mg/dL
Preprandial glucose level	Less than 100 mg/dL	60–99 mg/dL
Peak glucose level	No recommendation	100–129 mg/dL
Glucose level 1 hour after meals	Less than 140 mg/dL	No recommendation
Glucose level 2 hours after meals	Less than 120 mg/dL	No recommendation
Mean daily glucose level	100 mg/dL	Less than 110 mg/dL
Hemoglobin A_{1c} level	Less than 6%	Less than 6%

Data from Pregestational diabetes mellitus. ACOG Practice Bulletin No. 60. American College of Obstetricians and Gynecologists. Obstet Gynecol 2005;105:675–85 and Kitzmiller JL, Block JM, Brown FM, Catalano PM. Conway DL, Coustan DR, et al. Managing preexisting diabetes for pregnancy: summary of evidence and consensus recommendations for care. Diabetes Care 2008;31:1060–79.

women with diabetes mellitus are injecting more than 50 units of insulin at a time, they must use the 1-mL syringes, and dosage adjustments should be made in even numbers of units. Hypoglycemia is more frequent in pregnancy than at other times; this is especially true in early pregnancy, particularly in patients with type 1 diabetes mellitus. Some patients with long-standing diabetes mellitus develop "hypoglycemia unawareness," a condition in which the usual adrenergic responses to hypoglycemia (eg, shakiness and diaphoresis) do not occur, and the first sign may be slurred speech and confusion, loss of consciousness, or both. Typically, patients with this condition are not able to sense when their blood sugar levels are below 50–60 mg/dL. The patient and her family should be taught to respond rapidly to hypoglycemia with a mixed protein–carbohydrate snack. Although a pure carbohydrate snack is traditionally administered to hypoglycemic nonpregnant patients, protein is absorbed more slowly and is less likely to cause significant "overshoot" hyperglycemia, which may be harmful to the fetus. Family members should be given instructions on how to mix and inject glucagon when hypoglycemia renders the patient unconscious, unwilling, or unable to take a snack orally. Box 6 describes the method for mixing and injecting glucagon.

Table 4 lists various available types of insulin and their characteristics. None of the agents currently available have been

---

Box 6. Use of Glucagon to Treat Severe Hypoglycemia

- Glucagon should be used only when the patient is unable to take an oral snack and intravenous glucose is not available.

- Glucagon is supplied as a kit that contains a vial of sterile glucagon (1 mg) and a syringe with 1 mL of sterile diluting solution. The glucagon must be reconstituted before use. Once it is reconstituted, it should be used immediately.

- The glucagon kit can be stored at room temperature.

(continued)

Box 6. Use of Glucagon to Treat Severe Hypoglycemia *(continued)*

- Glucagon is reconstituted as follows:

  1. Remove the flip top seal from the bottle of glucagon powder. Wipe the rubber stopper with an alcohol swab.

  2. Remove the needle protector from the syringe. Inject the entire contents of the syringe into the bottle of glucagon powder. Do not remove the plastic clip from the syringe. Remove the syringe from the bottle.

  3. Swirl the bottle gently until glucagon dissolves completely and the solution is clear and of a water-like consistency.

  4. Using the same syringe, holding the bottle upside down, gently withdraw all of the solution (1 mg mark on the syringe) from the bottle. The usual adult dose is 1 mg (1 unit).

- Glucagon is injected as follows:

  1. Cleanse the injection site on the buttock, arm, or thigh with alcohol swab.

  2. Insert the needle into the loose tissue under the cleansed injection site and inject all of the glucagon solution. Apply light pressure against the injection site and withdraw the needle. Press an alcohol swab against the injection site.

  3. Turn the patient on her side to prevent her from choking if she vomits when she awakens (an unconscious patient usually will awaken within 15 minutes of the injection).

shown to cross the placenta in appreciable amounts or harm the fetus, although some new insulin analogs, such as detemir and glulisine, have not been evaluated as thoroughly as the others.

Because of increasing insulin resistance, dosage usually increases significantly as pregnancy progresses. No absolute upper limit exists regarding the dosage of insulin that may be prescribed. The necessary dosage should be used to maintain circulating glucose values within target ranges.

When the total injectable dose exceeds 100 units, it may be necessary to give two injections or an alternative is to use U-500 insulin. Only regular insulin is marketed at the U-500 concentration, so if short-acting insulin analogues are used, the patient must be prescribed regular insulin. Because syringes are marked for U-100 insulin, it is critical that patients are aware that the U-500 insulin is five times the concentration of the usual U-100 insulin, so that each unit demarcation on the U-100 syringe is equivalent to 5 units of U-500 insulin. Dosages should be written down and their equivalent marking on the syringe noted. For example, a patient who takes 150 units of U-500 regular insulin would draw up the U-500 insulin to the 30-unit mark on the U-100 syringe. Often the patient will be taking a mixture of short-acting and intermediate-acting insulin (eg, neutral protamine Hagedorn). Because intermediate-acting insulin is available only as U-100 insulin, the patient will need explicit instructions on how to draw up the appropriate dose. Because of the potential for overdose or underdose, instructions should be clear and written out. The patient should vocalize her understanding in a manner similar to the "read back-and-verify" protocol.

PREVENTION OF MATERNAL COMPLICATIONS

Patients who manifest any degree of diabetic retinopathy should have a dilated retinal examination at least once each trimester. Laser photocoagulation may be used if indicated during pregnancy. If urine protein excretion has not been quantified during preconception care, this should be accomplished as early in pregnancy as possible to establish whether diabetic nephropathy is present. Because preeclampsia does not occur before 20 weeks of gestation, a proteinuria level of more than 300 mg per 24 hours in the first half of pregnancy is diagnostic of underlying kidney disease. Because renal plasma flow increases as pregnancy progresses, patients with preexisting nephropathy often spill large amounts of protein in later gestation; such increases in the proteinuria level cannot necessarily be ascribed to preeclampsia. Conversely, patients whose protein excretion is normal before pregnancy or in the first half of pregnancy and who subsequently develop proteinuria most likely have preeclampsia. Patients with chronic hypertension are at an increased risk of preeclampsia and stillbirth as well as fetal growth restriction. They should be treated to control blood pressure with medications other than ACE inhibitors or angiotensin receptor blockers; typically β-blockers, calcium channel blockers, or methyldopa are used. Diabetic gastroparesis may worsen during pregnancy and cause continued nausea and vomiting even after the first trimester. Metoclopramide may be helpful for such patients. Patients with type 1 diabetes mellitus are more prone to diabetic ketoacidosis during pregnancy than at other times. Diabetic ketoacidosis carries a high fetal mortality risk and should be identified early and treated aggressively. Risk factors for diabetic ketoacidosis include infections, treatment with betamimetic tocolytics or corticosteroids, and lack of patient adherence to treatment. Diabetic ketoacidosis may occur at lower blood glucose levels in pregnant women than in nonpregnant women. Treatment is similar to that for diabetic ketoacidosis in nonpregnant individuals. Hydration with IV fluids, low-dose IV insulin, potassium supplementation, and treatment of underlying causes are all important steps. Maternal diabetic ketoacidosis often is associated with nonreassuring fetal heart rate patterns. Fetal condition generally returns to normal as the diabetic ketoacidosis is corrected. Generally, it is not appropriate to respond to the nonreassuring fetal heart rate pattern with immediate cesarean delivery. Surgery is quite dangerous for patients during an episode of diabetic ketoacidosis, and by the time the patient is well enough to tolerate a cesarean delivery the fetal heart rate pattern will most often have become reassuring.

OBSTETRIC MANAGEMENT

Accurate pregnancy dating is essential in managing diabetic pregnancy; it allows for appropriate timing of interventions, when necessary. The earlier a first-trimester ultrasound examination can be performed, the more accurate is the dating.

Although maternal diabetes mellitus does not increase the risk of aneuploidy, neither does it protect against this possibility. Therefore, women with diabetes mellitus should be offered the same options for aneuploidy screening as are other obstetric patients. Because diabetes mellitus may predispose the fetus to all congenital malformations, including neural tube defects, alpha-fetoprotein testing should be made available either as part of aneuploidy screening or as a stand-alone test if aneuploidy screening is declined. A specialized (detailed) ultrasound examination should be offered at 18–20 weeks of gestation because most major anomalies are detectable by such an examination. In addition, fetal echocardiography may be a useful adjunct. As mentioned earlier, increasing levels of HbA_{1c} are associated with increasing risks of anomalies. Prenatal diagnosis of major malformations may be helpful in continuing pregnancies by allowing counseling and planning with the appropriate consultants to optimize neonatal management.

Because glucose crosses the placenta freely by a process of facilitated diffusion and insulin does not, fetal hyperinsulinemia often results from poorly controlled diabetes and appears to cause a number of adverse outcomes. High levels of fetal insulin accelerate fetal growth, and fetal macrosomia is a frequent complication of maternal diabetes. Large infants of diabetic women are more prone to shoulder dystocia and Erb palsy than are similarly large infants of nondiabetic women. Also, they are more likely to require cesarean delivery or operative vaginal delivery or have shoulder dystocia. Conversely, diabetic pregnant women are at an increased risk of IUGR, especially when vascular complications, such as hypertension, nephropathy, or retinopathy, are present. Thus, it is useful to monitor fetal growth by means of periodic ultrasound examinations. Fetal growth should be assessed monthly beginning at 26 weeks of gestation (or even earlier when fetal growth restriction risk is increased). The final growth assessment can be performed close to the time of delivery when macrosomia is suspected to help make a decision regarding mode of delivery.

Antepartum fetal evaluation, including fetal movement counting, the nonstress test, the biophysical profile, and the contraction

stress test, when performed at appropriate intervals is a valuable
approach and can be used to monitor the pregnancies of women
with pregestational diabetes mellitus. Initiation of testing is appropriate for most patients at 32–34 weeks of gestation. However,
testing at earlier gestational ages may be warranted in some pregnancies that are complicated by additional high-risk conditions.
In response to a report of stillbirths even in patients with a reac-
tive nonstress test within 1 week of delivery (74), twice weekly
testing has been widely adopted. Daily fetal movement counting
is a simple technique for antepartum assessment that also should
be considered. However, if maternal glucose control deteriorates,
the fetal condition may change, and repeat testing for fetal well-
being may be indicated. Doppler velocimetry of the umbilical
artery may be useful in monitoring pregnancies with vascular
complications and poor fetal growth (68).

The appropriate time for delivery in diabetic pregnant women
should be individualized based on factors, such as adequacy of
glucose control, presence or absence of diabetic vasculopathy,
and past history. Ideally, when diabetic control is excellent
and no other adverse risk factors are present, delivery can be
accomplished at 39 weeks of gestation or beyond but no later
than the expected date of confinement. Measurable risks are
associated with delivery before 39 weeks of gestation, and these
risks of early term or late preterm birth are greater in diabetic
patients than in nondiabetic patients. However, these risks must
be balanced against the risk of stillbirth when diabetes is poorly
controlled or when other problems, such as fetal growth restriction or preeclampsia supervene. The College recommends that an
amniocentesis for fetal lung maturity be performed for delivery
before 39 weeks of gestation (68). However, recommendations
from a 2011 workshop sponsored by the *Eunice Kennedy Shriver*
National Institute of Child Health and Human Development
(NICHD) and the Society for Maternal-Fetal Medicine (SMFM)
advocate that, in general, when an indication for delivery is present, the use of amniocentesis to assess fetal lung maturity would
not assist in guiding management (75). In the specific case of pregestational diabetes mellitus, it was recommended that delivery
before 39 weeks of gestation is not necessary when the diabetes is

well controlled, but if vascular disease is present, delivery should be accomplished at 37–39 weeks of gestation. When the diabetes is poorly controlled, delivery should be performed at 34–39 weeks of gestation, depending on the particular situation. Amniocentesis was not recommended for any of these scenarios.

The College recommends that cesarean delivery (without labor) be considered if the estimated fetal weight is greater than 4,500 g in women with diabetes mellitus to prevent traumatic birth injury (68). A decision analysis concluded that when the estimated fetal weight was 4,500 g or more in a diabetic pregnancy, 443 elective cesarean deliveries would be required to prevent one case of permanent brachial plexus injury (76). If elective cesarean deliveries were performed whenever the estimated fetal weight was 4,000 g or more, 489 operations would prevent one permanent brachial plexus injury (76).

The goal of diabetes management during labor is to avoid hyperglycemia, thus avoiding fetal hyperinsulinemia at the time of birth with resultant neonatal hypoglycemia. When labor begins spontaneously, subcutaneous insulin should be withheld and an IV infusion should be started, using 5% dextrose to provide for the energy requirements of labor and avoid starvation ketosis. Glucose level should be measured hourly. The goal should be to achieve a maternal glucose level in the range from 70 mg/dL to 120 mg/dL. If the maternal glucose level exceeds the goal, regular insulin is added to the IV line at a rate of 1–1.25 units per hour. Generally, it takes 4 hours to reach a steady state, and in the meantime the insulin dose can be adjusted up or down depending on the trend in glucose levels.

When labor induction is planned, the patient is instructed to eat dinner and take her usual insulin dose the night before induction. Labor induction is scheduled as early the next morning as is practical, subcutaneous insulin is withheld, and the patient does not eat. An IV glucose infusion is started as described previously, and insulin is added to the IV line as necessary. For planned cesarean delivery, assuming a maternal glucose level is in the target range at the time of surgery, IV normal saline solution or lactated Ringer solution can be infused until the infant is delivered, at which time the infusion can be changed to 5% glucose.

POSTPARTUM CARE

Insulin requirements usually decrease rapidly once the infant and placenta have been delivered. If type 1 diabetes mellitus was well controlled before conception, the patient may be given her prepregnancy insulin dose once she is able to eat. Patients with type 2 diabetes mellitus who were using oral antidiabetic agents before pregnancy may resume taking these drugs after delivery. The postpartum period provides an excellent opportunity for preconception counseling for the next pregnancy. In addition, most women with diabetes are able to achieve much better control of their glucose values during pregnancy than they had experienced previously. The success of achieving good control during pregnancy can be used as a "teachable moment" to reinforce lifetime skills and habits of diabetes mellitus management.

LACTATION

The woman with preexisting diabetes mellitus should be encouraged to breastfeed her infant. Lactation requires ingestion of an additional 500 kcal per day, and control of diabetes mellitus may be easier during lactation. Breastfed infants are less likely to develop type 1 diabetes mellitus than are bottle-fed infants. Breastfeeding also has been shown to decrease the likelihood of a number of childhood infectious diseases. The incidence rates of childhood atopic eczema, celiac disease, and sudden infant death syndrome also appear to be reduced, along with the possible reduction of asthma and ulcerative colitis rates. Glyburide, metformin, and acarbose appear to be minimally transferred into breast milk and can be used by lactating women. More complete information on this topic may be found in the section "Breastfeeding and Diabetes" in *Managing Preexisting Diabetes and Pregnancy: Technical Reviews and Consensus Recommendations for Care*, listed in the section "Resources" in this monograph.

FAMILY PLANNING

Contraception for women with diabetes mellitus is discussed earlier in this monograph. Women who breastfeed their offspring often have questions about appropriate contraceptive methods.

Ovulation has been documented to occur as early as 25 days after delivery. Women who are exclusively breastfeeding are unlikely to ovulate for the first 6 months or so. However, if breastfeeding is supplemented with any other source of nutrition or hydration and immediate pregnancy is not desired, earlier use of contraception should be considered. Hormonal contraception is compatible with breastfeeding because very little of the hormones is present in breast milk. Because it is not clear whether combination oral contraception decreases the volume of milk early in the course of lactation, the College recommends that the use of combination oral contraceptives may be considered once milk flow has been established (77). This also should allow enough time to pass for the hypercoagulable state present in postpartum women to have abated; for nonlactating women, the recommendation is to wait 4 weeks. Progestin-only pills and DMPA do not interfere with breastfeeding and do not have a procoagulant effect. The College's recommendation follows the product labeling to initiate DMPA or progestin-only pills at 6 weeks in lactating women and immediately postpartum in nonlactating women.

■ **CASE NO. 4.** A 24-year-old nulliparous patient who has type 2 diabetes mellitus, infertility, and PCOS has a BMI of 40. She is being treated with metformin and presents at 8 weeks of gestation for an initial prenatal visit. She is interested in learning how her pregnancy will be managed and whether she needs to continue the metformin now that she has successfully conceived.

A thorough history should be obtained, including an assessment of recent diabetic control by measurement of HbA_{1c} levels and review of any self-glucose monitoring records. The presence or absence of nephropathy should be determined and the patient should be referred for dilated retinal examination if none has been performed recently. Routine prenatal laboratory testing also should be performed. In addition, because of the increased risk of preeclampsia in diabetic pregnancy, it would be worthwhile to measure baseline liver enzyme levels and the serum creatinine level at this early stage for later comparison should hypertension develop. The patient should be counseled regarding the risk of congenital malformations in diabetic pregnancy and the risk estimate should be tailored in accordance with the patient's initial HbA_{1c} level. If her level is high, it may be worthwhile to institute rapid improvement of diabetic control, even including inpatient care if necessary because organogenesis is still ongoing. The patient should be informed of the pathophysiology of maternal–fetal hyperglycemia leading to fetal hyperinsulinemia, and in turn, adverse outcomes, using terminology that is appropriate to the patient's level of understanding. Appropriate prenatal diagnostic approaches should be offered, and the overall management plan for fetal evaluation and testing as pregnancy progresses should be outlined. It is important to schedule a first-trimester ultrasound examination to establish the correct dating of the pregnancy, particularly in patients who conceive after treatment for anovulatory disorders because the date of the last menstrual period may not be very helpful. If planned delivery is necessary toward the end of pregnancy, having an accurate estimated date of confinement is critical. The patient should meet with members of the team who provide care for diabetes in pregnancy. A nutritionist should counsel the patient regarding an appropriate diet for her pregnancy. A diabetes nurse educator can teach the patient about self-glucose monitoring at least four times daily (fasting and either 1 hour or 2 hours after meals). She should be advised to discontinue metformin because it crosses the placenta and fetal effects are unknown. An insulin regimen should be initiated as necessary, and frequent contact should be planned to achieve near-euglycemia.

Gestational Diabetes Mellitus

EPIDEMIOLOGY

Gestational diabetes mellitus is defined as carbohydrate intolerance with an onset or first recognition during pregnancy. Although differences in diagnostic criteria, screening paradigms, and reporting make ascertainment of population prevalence difficult and comparisons impossible, it is clear that the prevalence of GDM has been increasing markedly in recent years, most likely related to the epidemic of obesity noted earlier in this monograph.

A survey of national hospital discharge diagnoses, which are typically underreported, found that the diagnosis of GDM was recorded for 2.9% of all deliveries in 1994, and had increased by 56% to 4.6% of all deliveries by 2004 (71). In a report based on data from a universally screened multiethnic population in Colorado, the diagnosis of GDM doubled from 2.1% to 4.1% between 1994 and 2002 (78). Similar increases were found for all ethnic groups and were still present when the data were adjusted for maternal age. In this population, the National Diabetes Data Group criteria were used for the diagnosis of GDM; one would expect significantly higher prevalence to have been present if the Carpenter–Coustan criteria had been used (Table 6). It is also true that Colorado has consistently had the lowest prevalence of obesity of any state, such that higher prevalences would be expected in other parts of the country.

MATERNAL, FETAL, AND NEONATAL EFFECTS

Gestational diabetes mellitus clearly is a marker for increased risk of subsequent type 2 diabetes mellitus. In addition, women with GDM are more likely to experience hypertensive disorders of pregnancy and cesarean delivery. The fetus of a woman with GDM is prone to stillbirth and macrosomia with the attendant risks of shoulder dystocia and birth injury. The neonate is more likely to experience complications of prematurity and, even if born at term, hyperbilirubinemia and hypoglycemia. All or most

Table 6. Diagnostic Criteria for Gestational Diabetes, Using the 100-g, 3-Hour Oral Glucose Tolerance Test

	Plasma or Serum Glucose (mg/dL)	
Time of sample	Carpenter–Coustan Conversion	National Diabetes Data Group Conversion
Fasting	95	105
1 hour	180	190
2 hours	155	165
3 hours	140	145

Gestational diabetes is diagnosed when any two or more of the thresholds are met or exceeded.
Modified from Gestational diabetes. ACOG Practice Bulletin No. 30. American College of Obstetricians and Gynecologists. Obstet Gynecol 2001;98:525–38.

of these potential problems appear to be related to fetal hyperinsulinemia, which results from maternal–fetal hyperglycemia.

SCREENING

The College recommends that all pregnant women be screened for GDM. Screening can consist of using historical risk factors, but most obstetricians screen all pregnant patients using a laboratory determination of plasma glucose level 1 hour after a 50-g glucose challenge at 24–28 weeks of gestation. Earlier testing is appropriate when the risk of GDM is high as in women with previous GDM. The test can be administered without regard to the time of the last meal. Capillary glucose testing with meters and test strips is neither precise nor accurate enough for screening and diagnostic testing. The threshold for further testing is either 140 mg/dL (80% sensitivity) or 130 mg/dL (90% or more sensitivity).

DIAGNOSIS

The College recommends that GDM be diagnosed using a 100-g, 3-hour OGTT. The plasma or serum glucose level is measured in a laboratory. Two alternative sets of diagnostic criteria are offered by the College. Both are conversions from the original O'Sullivan criteria (venous whole blood samples) to plasma and more up-to-date measurement technology. Values for both are shown in Table 6.

MANAGEMENT

Medical management of GDM is similar to that outlined earlier for preexisting diabetes mellitus in pregnancy. The goal is to maintain glucose levels that minimize the likelihood of fetal hyperinsulinemia. Self-glucose monitoring is performed while fasting and either 1 hour or 2 hours after each meal. Goals are as follows:

- Fasting, 95 mg/dL or less
- 1-hour, 130–140 mg/dL or less
- 2-hour, 120 mg/dL or less

When these goals are not attained with medical nutrition therapy alone, therapy with insulin should be considered. A randomized trial that compared use of metformin and insulin in patients with GDM that required treatment demonstrated similar outcomes in each treatment group (79). However, nearly one half of the patients randomized to treatment with metformin required the addition of insulin. No adverse effects of metformin on pregnancy outcomes were observed, but long-term follow-up of the offspring is yet to be reported. As noted in the section that discusses use of oral antidiabetic agents in preexisting diabetic pregnancy, the College recommends that the use of these drugs be limited and individualized until more data regarding safety and efficacy become available (68). Many patients with GDM can be treated successfully with diet alone, and often their frequency of self-glucose monitoring can be safely reduced to every other day. Randomized trials have demonstrated that the measurement of fetal abdominal circumference in the early third trimester can help inform the decision to start insulin therapy (80).

No consensus exists regarding the need for, frequency of, or type of antepartum fetal testing most appropriate for women with GDM. The risks of adverse outcomes described earlier for patients with preexisting diabetes in pregnancy are similar in nature, but lower in magnitude with GDM, particularly when glucose values are near normal without the need for insulin. The College indicates, "despite the lack of conclusive data, it would seem reasonable that women whose GDM is not well controlled, who require insulin, or have other risk factors should be managed the same as individuals with preexisting diabetes" (81). Estimation of fetal weight at or near the time of delivery is helpful in guiding decision making regarding mode of delivery. Evidence suggests that ultrasonography is no more accurate than clinical estimation (82). The same considerations regarding macrosomia and potential shoulder dystocia hold for GDM as for preexisting diabetes mellitus. As described earlier, discussion of cesarean delivery without labor is suggested when the estimated fetal weight is 4,500 g or more. When the estimated fetal weight is 4,000–4,500 g, other factors should be taken into consideration, including previous deliveries, clinical pelvimetry, and the progress of labor.

The workshop sponsored by NICHD and SMFM recommended that later preterm or early term delivery is not necessary when GDM is well controlled by diet or insulin (75). When GDM is poorly controlled, delivery between 34 weeks of gestation and 39 weeks of gestation, individualized to the situation, was suggested. Management during labor should be aimed toward maintaining euglycemia as described in the section "Preexisting Diabetes Mellitus."

Patients with GDM, including those who required insulin during pregnancy, should not require antidiabetic medication after delivery, unless they are found to have previously undiscovered type 2 diabetes mellitus (or in rare circumstances type 1 diabetes). Although diabetes mellitus and prediabetes can be diagnosed on the basis of a fasting plasma glucose level alone, or a HbA_{1c} level alone, neither of these approaches will establish the diagnosis of impaired glucose tolerance, a form of prediabetes. Because, by definition, women who have recently completed a pregnancy complicated by GDM are still in their childbearing years, and a subsequent pregnancy is a possibility, establishing the diagnosis of prediabetes is clinically significant. Because patients with prediabetes may subsequently develop diabetes mellitus before conception and need prepregnancy counseling as described earlier for preexisting diabetes, a 75-g, 2-hour OGTT at the time of the postpartum visit, is appropriate. Diagnostic criteria are described in Table 1. Issues related to lactation and family planning are discussed earlier in the section "Preexisting Diabetes Mellitus."

 Concerns for Older Women

The NHANES data from 2005–2008 revealed that 27% of adults aged 65 years and older have diagnosed or undiagnosed diabetes (1). That proportion is expected to continue to increase as the population ages. Compared with older patients without diabetes mellitus, those with diabetes mellitus have a higher likelihood of coexisting illnesses, premature death, and functional impairment. Stroke, hypertension, and heart disease are particularly likely. Additional problems include cognitive impairment, incontinence, falls, and depression. The American Geriatric Society has published guidelines for diabetes mellitus care in older individuals (see "Resources"). The ADA recommends that older individuals who meet certain requirements (ie, are functional, cognitively intact, and have significant life expectancy) should receive diabetes mellitus care in accordance with goals developed for younger adults (26). Goals for glycemic control may be relaxed when these requirements are not met, but symptomatic hyperglycemia should still be avoided. Treatment of hypertension is appropriate for all older adults, although lipid treatment and aspirin therapy may be of benefit when life expectancy is at least equal to the time frame of prevention trials, usually 10 years. Older patients are more likely to have kidney or heart failure, which contraindicates the use of metformin. Thiazolidinediones are contraindicated in the presence of congestive heart failure because they may cause fluid retention. Insulin and secretogogues may cause hypoglycemia; insulin requires the ability to draw up the proper dosage, although this may be accomplished by a caregiver when the patient is unable to do so. Older patients may require lower doses of many medications than doses required by the general population, and may be more prone to adverse effects.

CASE NO. 5. An 81-year-old woman comes in for care. She is accompanied by her 55-year-old daughter who lives with her, has type 2 diabetes mellitus, and is your gynecologic patient. The older patient has not seen a physician for the past 35 years, and screening at the local senior center revealed a random blood glucose level of 385 mg/dL.

The initial evaluation should include components outlined earlier in this monograph. In older patients, particular attention should be paid to mental status and comorbidities. This patient manifests a blood pressure of 170 mm Hg, systolic, and 100 mm Hg, diastolic, and her electrocardiogram shows evidence of an old posterior myocardial infarction. Her BMI is 38. Her serum creatinine level is 1.3 mg/dL and her urine shows 2+ protein. Her HDL cholesterol level is 38 mg/dL, and her low-density lipoprotein cholesterol level is 150 mg/dL with a triglyceride level of 210 mg/dL.

She is somewhat disoriented and her daughter tells you that she has become very forgetful over the past 2 years. You suggest referral to a gerontologist for primary care management, and the daughter asks you what the treatment is likely to be. You explain that the patient has evidence of type 2 diabetes mellitus, coronary heart disease, renal impairment, and probable cognitive impairment. Although she will need further evaluation of these problems, it is likely that she will be prescribed medical nutrition therapy and oral antidiabetic medications with the goal of preventing chronic severe hyperglycemia, although, in view of her apparent mental status impairment and comorbidities, it is not the near normalization that the daughter is aiming for. The particular medications prescribed will depend on an evaluation of renal and cardiac functions. Her hypertension should be treated, and she should probably be administered a statin. Although her life expectancy appears to be limited, her previous myocardial infarction means that the lipid lowering treatment is secondary rather than primary prevention, and thus, is appropriate despite her age and comorbidities. She and her daughter, who is her primary caregiver, will both need counseling and assistance in maintaining a reasonable quality of life, which will be the primary goal.

Complementary and Alternative Medicine

According to the National Center for Complementary and Alternative Medicine (NCCAM), complementary and alternative medicine (CAM) is defined as "a group of diverse medical and health care systems, practices, and products that are not generally considered to be part of conventional medicine." The use of CAM is increasing, and the NIH maintains a web site (see "Resources") that provides information from the NCCAM. Scientific information about CAM and diabetes mellitus is scanty. The following information comes from the NCCAM's web site:

- Chromium picolinate: A double-blind, cross-over, placebo-controlled randomized trial of either 500 micrograms or

1,000 micrograms daily in 59 adults with prediabetes or metabolic syndrome found no significant improvement in characteristics, which would be expected to reduce the risk of developing type 2 diabetes mellitus.

- Omega-3 fatty acids: A review of published evidence conducted by the Agency for Healthcare Research and Quality found that among 18 studies of type 2 diabetes mellitus or metabolic syndrome, omega-3 fatty acid supplementation improved triglyceride levels (compared with placebo) but had no effect on total cholesterol, HDL cholesterol, fasting glucose or HbA_{1c} level, or on plasma insulin level or insulin resistance.

- Alpha-lipoic acid: This antioxidant is found in food, such as liver, spinach, broccoli, and potatoes. Some studies have found that it benefits insulin sensitivity and diabetic neuropathy, but the data are inconclusive. Patients with diabetes mellitus who take alpha-lipoic acid need to monitor their blood sugar levels to be sure they are not too low.

- Polyphenols: These antioxidants are found in tea and dark chocolate. Laboratory studies suggested that EGCG, an antioxidant found in green tea, may protect against CV disease and improve insulin sensitivity and glucose control. Clinical studies in patients with diabetes mellitus have failed to demonstrate such benefits. Green tea is safe in moderation.

- Garlic: This has not been shown to decrease blood glucose levels consistently.

- Magnesium: Eating a diet high in magnesium may decrease the risk of developing diabetes.

- Coenzyme Q10: Study results regarding improving glucose control have been inconsistent.

- Ginseng: Currently under study.

- Vanadium: Currently under study.

- Botanicals (eg, prickly pear cactus, gurmar, aloe vera, fenugreek, or bitter melon): Limited data.

Patients with diabetes mellitus are advised not to use CAM treatments that are unproven as a substitute for scientifically proven treatments for diabetes mellitus. Also, they should be aware that labeling of dietary supplements may not always be accurate. The NCCAM is currently funding a number of ongoing studies of these therapies and further information will likely become available.

Drug Interactions

A useful reference on drug–drug interactions for medications commonly used to treat diabetes and their complications may be found on the ADA's web site (see "Resources"). A few of the most salient interactions are listed as follows:

• Sulfonylureas: These drugs are metabolized by the cytochrome P450 isozyme 2C9 (CYP2C9). Their levels may be increased by concomitant use of CYP2C9 inhibitors, such as fluconazole, trimethoprim, amiodarone, and reduced by concomitant use of inducers of CYP2C9, such as rifampin and phenobarbital. Sulfonylureas are metabolized by the liver and eliminated by the kidneys and in feces. Impairment of hepatic or renal function may change their efficacy.

• Metformin: Cimetidine may compete for renal elimination so levels of metformin may increase. Lactic acidosis may occur, particularly in the case of concomitant renal impairment or hypoxia.

• Angiotensin-converting enzyme inhibitors and angiotensin receptor blockers: Captopril is metabolized by the cytochrome P450 isozyme 2D6. Its levels may increase when used concomitantly with inhibitors of this isozyme, such as cimetidine, fluoxetine, and paroxetine. Enalapril is metabolized by the cytochrome P450 isozyme 3A4. Levels may be increased by inhibitors of this isozyme, such as erythromycin or clarithromycin (but not azithromycin), verapamil, diltiazem, ketoconazole, fluoxetine, and HIV protease inhibitors. Levels may be decreased by concomitant use with inducers of this isozyme, including carbamazepine, rifampin, phenobarbital, and phenytoin. The antihypertensive effects of ACE inhibitors may be reduced by the concomitant use of aspirin or nonsteroidal antiinflammatory drugs, and increased by the use of lithium. Angiotensin-converting enzyme inhibitors and angiotensin receptor blockers should not be used in pregnancy.

- Calcium channel blockers: These drugs are inhibitors of the cytochrome P450 isozyme 3A4, and their use may increase concentrations of drugs metabolized by this isozyme, such as enalapril and losartan.

Conclusions and Future Directions

It is clear that diabetes is present and ever-growing in a proportion of the population and adds significantly to health care costs and detracts significantly from life expectancy and quality of life. Many new developments can be anticipated in the years to come. The place of continuous glucose monitoring in the management of diabetes is still to be established. New drugs that act by new mechanisms are likely to emerge. Also, new developments can be anticipated in the approach to the delivery of health care to patients with diabetes.

One recent development is a recommendation for new diagnostic criteria for GDM that use a 75-g, 2-hour OGTT. The International Association of Diabetes in Pregnancy Study Groups has recommended that if any one or more of the following values is met or exceeded, GDM is present (83):

- Fasting plasma glucose level, 92 mg/dL
- 1-hr plasma glucose level, 180 mg/dL
- 2-hr plasma glucose level, 153 mg/dL

Professional groups around the world are now considering these recommendations. If they are adopted universally, outcome-based criteria that are uniform will allow comparison from one population to another. However, the change from requiring two elevated values to only one elevated value for the diagnosis, along with the decrease of the glucose load, will lead to a marked increase in the proportion of pregnant women with GDM. It is likely that the new criteria will identify 16–18% of the population. Although this may seem excessive for a disease, it should be considered in the context of population statistics that more than one third of adult Americans have either diabetes mellitus or prediabetes. The proposed thresholds for GDM are not too dissimilar from the thresholds for prediabetes in the nonpregnant individual. Because the fasting plasma glucose level decreases in pregnancy, the cutoff of 92 mg/dL is not so different from the 100 mg/dL cutoff for an impaired fasting glucose level. The 2-hr threshold of 153 mg/dL is actually higher than the 140 mg/dL cutoff on a 2-hour OGTT used to diagnose impaired glucose tolerance. Thus, the diagnostic criteria for GDM proposed by the International Association of Diabetes in Pregnancy Study Groups may identify a similar population to that with prediabetes by using standard criteria for nonpregnant individuals. The ADA has endorsed these new diagnostic criteria, whereas the College suggests awaiting further data (84).

Resources

Publications

Gestational diabetes. ACOG Practice Bulletin No. 30. American College of Obstetricians and Gynecologists. Obstet Gynecol 2001;98:525–38.

Pregestational diabetes mellitus. ACOG Practice Bulletin No. 60. American College of Obstetricians and Gynecologists. Obstet Gynecol 2005;105: 675–85.

Use of hormonal contraception in women with coexisting medical conditions. ACOG Practice Bulletin No. 73. American College of Obstetricians and Gynecologists. Obstet Gynecol 2006;107:1453–72.

The following resources are for information purposes only. Referral to these sources and web sites does not imply the endorsement of the American College of Obstetricians and Gynecologists. These resources are not meant to be comprehensive. The exclusion of a source or web site does not reflect the quality of that source or web site. Please note that web sites are subject to change without notice.

Bantle JP, Wylie-Rosett J, Albright AL, Apovian CM, Clark NG, Franz MJ, et al. Nutrition recommendations and interventions for diabetes: a position statement of the American Diabetes Association. American Diabetes Association [published erratum appears in Diabetes Care 2010;33:1911]. Diabetes Care 2008;31 Suppl 1:S61–78.

Diagnosis and classification of diabetes mellitus. American Diabetes Association. Diabetes Care 2012;35 Suppl 1:S64–71.

Standards of Medical Care in Diabetes--2012. American Diabetes Association. Diabetes Care 2012;35 Suppl 1:S11–63.

Triplitt C. Drug interactions of medications commonly used in diabetes. Diabetes Spectr 2006;19:202–11.

Rasmussen KM, Yaktine AL, editors. Weight gain during pregnancy: reexamining the guidelines. Washington, D.C. National Academies Press; 2009. Available at: http://www.iom.edu/Reports/2009/Weight-Gain-During-Pregnancy-Reexamining-the-Guidelines.aspx. Retrieved January 15, 2013.

National diabetes fact sheet: national estimates and general information about diabetes and prediabetes in the United States, 2011. Centers for Disease Control and Prevention. Atlanta (GA): CDC; 2011. Available at: http://www.cdc.gov/diabetes/pubs/pdf/ndfs_2011.pdf. Retrieved January 8, 2013.

Bariatric surgery for severe obesity. Bethesda (MD): National Institute of Diabetes and Digestive and Kidney Diseases; 2009. p. 6. Available at http://win.niddk.nih.gov/publications/PDFs/Bariatric_Surgery_508.pdf. Retrieved January 15, 2013.

(continued)

Resources *(continued)*

Kitzmiller JL, Jovanovic L, Brown F, Coustan D, Reader DM, editors. Managing preexisting diabetes and pregnancy: technical reviews and consensus recommendations for care. Alexandria (VA): American Diabetes Association; 2008.

2008 physical activity guidelines for Americans: be active, healthy, and happy! Washington, DC: U.S. Dept. of Health and Human Services; 2008. Available at: http://www.health.gov/paguidelines/pdf/paguide.pdf. Retrieved May 16, 2013.

Web Sites and Online Tools

American Diabetes Association
Estimated average glucose calculator
professional.diabetes.org/GlucoseCalculator.aspx

American Geriatrics Society
www.americangeriatrics.org

National Institutes of Health: National Center for Complementary and Alternative Medicine
nccam.nih.gov

National Institute of Diabetes and Digestive and Kidney Diseases
www2.niddk.nih.gov

Information resource regarding complementary and alternative medicine for diabetes
diabetes.niddk.nih.gov/dm/pubs/alternativetherapies/

National Kidney Disease Education Program
Glomerular filtration rate calculator
www.nkdep.nih.gov/lab-evaluation/gfr-calculators.shtml

U.S. Department of Health and Human Services
www.hhs.gov

YMCA
Diabetes Prevention Program
www.ymca.net/diabetes-prevention/

Test Your Clinical Skills

Complete the answer sheet at the back of this book and return it to the American College of Obstetricians and Gynecologists to receive Continuing Medical Education credits. The answers appear on page 92.

Directions: Select the one best answer or completion.

1. Currently, what percentage of the U.S. population has diabetes mellitus or prediabetes?
   A. 11%
   B. 21%
   C. 35%
   D. 46%

2. In the pancreas, the direct activity of the glucokinase gene probably controls
   A. insulin secretion
   B. insulin resistance
   C. glucose sensing
   D. glucose entry into cells

3. In the United States in 2010, the ethnic group with the highest rate of diabetes was
   A. Asian
   B. Hispanic
   C. non-Hispanic white
   D. non-Hispanic black

4. A patient with an HbA_{1c} level of 5.6% has what probability of developing diabetes in the next 5 years?
   A. 1–10%
   B. 10–15%
   C. 9–25%
   D. 25–50%

5. An HbA_{1c} level of 6% suggests an estimated average glucose level (mg/dL) in the
   A. 120s
   B. 130s
   C. 140s
   D. 150s

6. The most common adverse effect of metformin is
   A. GI upset
   B. hypoglycemia
   C. lactic acidosis
   D. renal impairment

7. A patient who takes rosiglitazone, which results in reduction of the HbA_{1c} level from 8% to 6%, can expect her weight to
   A. decrease 4–6 lb
   B. decrease 9–13 lb
   C. increase 4–6 lb
   D. increase 9–13 lb

8. Which of the following peptides is produced in the pancreas?
   A. Amylin
   B. Glucagon-like peptide-1
   C. Gastric inhibitory polypeptide
   D. Dipeptidyl peptidase 4

9. In patients with type 2 diabetes mellitus, retinal changes can be seen as early as
   A. 5 years before diagnosis
   B. at the time of diagnosis
   C. 5 years after diagnosis
   D. 7 years after diagnosis

10. Treatment of diabetic ketoacidosis begins with the administration of
    A. 5% dextrose
    B. normal saline solution
    C. insulin, 10 units per hour
    D. potassium

11. A patient in the first trimester of pregnancy has an HbA_{1c} level of 9.8%. The risk of fetal anomaly in this pregnancy is
    A. 3%
    B. 6%
    C. 10 %
    D. 20%

12. A pregnant woman with type 1 diabetes mellitus weighs
    220 lb. Her daily intake should be
    A. 1,200 kcal
    B. 1,800 kcal
    C. 2,400 kcal
    D. 2,800 kcal

13. During labor, a patient with pregestational diabetes mellitus
    should have a blood glucose level of
    A. 50–80 mg/dL
    B. 60–100 mg/dL
    C. 70–120 mg/dL
    D. 120–140 mg/dL

14. The authors recommend that postpartum management of
    patients with GDM includes
    A. no further glucose testing
    B. obtaining results from an HbA_{1c} test
    C. obtaining results from a fasting glucose test
    D. obtaining results from 2-hr OGTT

15. Review of studies that involved omega-3 fatty acid supple-
    mentation in type 2 diabetes mellitus found improvement in
    A. HDL cholesterol levels
    B. HbA_{1c} levels
    C. triglyceride levels
    D. total cholesterol levels

References

1. National diabetes fact sheet: national estimates and general information about diabetes and prediabetes in the United States, 2011. Centers for Disease Control and Prevention. Atlanta (GA): CDC; 2011. Available at: http://www.cdc.gov/diabetes/pubs/pdf/ndfs_2011.pdf. Retrieved January 8, 2012. (Level III)

2. Cowie CC, Rust KF, Byrd-Holt DD, Eberhardt MS, Flegal KM, Engelgau MM, et al. Prevalence of diabetes and impaired fasting glucose in adults in the U.S. population: National Health And Nutrition Examination Survey 1999-2002. Diabetes Care 2006;29:1263–8. (Level II-3)

3. Diagnosis and classification of diabetes mellitus. American Diabetes Association. Diabetes Care 2012;35 Suppl 1:S64–71. (Level III)

4. Stumvoll M, Goldstein BJ, van Haeften TW. Type 2 diabetes: principles of pathogenesis and therapy. Lancet 2005;365:1333–46. (Level III)

5. Kahn CR. Banting lecture. Insulin action, diabetogenes, and the cause of type II diabetes. Diabetes 1994;43:1066–84. (Level III)

6. Weyer C, Bogardus C, Mott DM, Pratley RE. The natural history of insulin secretory dysfunction and insulin resistance in the pathogenesis of type 2 diabetes mellitus. J Clin Invest 1999;104:787–94. (Level III)

7. Barnett AH, Eff C, Leslie RD, Pyke DA: Diabetes in identical twins. A study of 200 pairs. Diabetologia 1981;20:87–93. (Level III)

8. Billings LK, Florez JC. The genetics of type 2 diabetes: what have we learned from GWAS? Ann N Y Acad Sci 2010;1212:59–77. (Level III)

9. Grundy SM, Cleeman JI, Daniels SR, Donato KA, Eckel RH, Franklin BA, et al. Diagnosis and management of the metabolic syndrome: an American Heart Association/National Heart, Lung, and Blood Institute Scientific Statement. American Heart Association and National Heart, Lung, and Blood Institute [published errata appear in Circulation 2005;112:e297. Circulation 2005;112:e298]. Circulation 2005;112:2735–52. (Level III)

10. Ervin RB. Prevalence of metabolic syndrome among adults 20 years of age and over, by sex, age, race and ethnicity, and body mass index: United States, 2003-2006. Natl Health Stat Report 2009;(13):1–7. (Level II-3)

11. Fajans SS, Bell GI, Polonsky KS. Molecular mechanisms and clinical pathophysiology of maturity-onset diabetes in the young. N Engl J Med 2001;345:971–80. (Level III)

12. Luna B, Feinglos MN. Drug-induced hyperglycemia. JAMA 2001;286:1945–8. (Level III)

13. Gurwitz JH, Bohn RL, Glynn RJ, Monane M, Mogun H, Avorn J. Glucocorticoids and the risk for initiation of hypoglycemic therapy. Arch Intern Med 1994;154:97–101. (Level II-3)

14. Goldfine AB. Statins: is it really time to reassess benefits and risks? N Engl J Med 2012;366:1752–5. (Level III)

15. Pavkov ME, Hanson RL, Knowler WC, Bennett PH, Krakoff J, Nelson RG. Changing patterns of type 2 diabetes incidence among Pima Indians. Diabetes Care 2007;30:1758–63. (Level II-3)

16. Gale EA, Gillespie KM. Diabetes and gender. Diabetologia 2001;44:3–15. (Level III)

17. Bingley PJ, Douek IF, Rogers CA, Gale EA. Influence of maternal age at delivery and birth order on risk of type 1 diabetes in childhood: prospective population based family study. Bart's-Oxford Family Study Group. BMJ 2000;321:420–4. (Level II-2)

18. Kuczmarski RJ, Flegal KM, Campbell SM, Johnson CL. Increasing prevalence of overweight among US adults. The National Health and Nutrition Examination Surveys, 1960 to 1991. JAMA 1994;272:205–11. (Level II-3)

19. Flegal KM, Carroll MD, Ogden CL, Curtin LR. Prevalence and trends in obesity among US adults, 1999-2008. JAMA 2010;303:235–41. (Level II-3)

20. Flegal KM, Carroll MD, Kit BK, Ogden CL. Prevalence of obesity and trends in the distribution of body mass index among US adults, 1999-2010. JAMA 2012;307:491–7. (Level II-3)

21. Norris JM, Barriga K, Klingensmith G, Hoffman M, Eisenbarth GS, Erlich HA, et al. Timing of initial cereal exposure in infancy and risk of islet autoimmunity. JAMA 2003;290:1713–20. (Level II-2)

22. Akerblom HK, Krischer J, Virtanen SM, Berseth C, Becker D, Dupre J, et al. The Trial to Reduce IDDM in the Genetically at Risk (TRIGR) study: recruitment, intervention and follow-up. TRIGR Study Group. Diabetologia 2011; 54:627–33. (Level I)

23. Knowler WC, Barrett-Connor E, Fowler SE, Hamman RF, Lachin JM, Walker EA, et al. Reduction in the incidence of type 2 diabetes with lifestyle intervention or metformin. Diabetes Prevention Program Research Group. N Engl J Med 2002;346:393–403. (Level I)

24. Gerstein HC, Yusuf S, Bosch J, Pogue J, Sheridan P, Dinccag N, et al. Effect of rosiglitazone on the frequency of diabetes in patients with impaired glucose tolerance or impaired fasting glucose: a randomised controlled trial. DREAM (Diabetes Reduction Assessment with ramipril and rosiglitazone Medication) Trial Investigators [published erratum appears in Lancet 2006; 368:1770]. Lancet 2006;368:1096–105. (Level I)

25. Zhang X, Gregg EW, Williamson DF, Barker LE, Thomas W, Bullard KM, et al. A1C level and future risk of diabetes: a systematic review. Diabetes Care 2010; 33:1665–73. (Level III)

26. Standards of Medical Care in Diabetes--2012. American Diabetes Association. Diabetes Care 2012;35 Suppl 1:S11–63. (Level III)

27. Funnell MM, Brown TL, Childs BP, Haas LB, Hosey GM, Jensen B, et al. National standards for diabetes self-management education. Diabetes Care 2012;35 Suppl 1:S101–8. (Level III)

28. Bantle JP, Wylie-Rosett J, Albright AL, Apovian CM, Clark NG, Franz MJ, et al. Nutrition recommendations and interventions for diabetes: a position statement of the American Diabetes Association. American Diabetes Association [published erratum appears in Diabetes Care 2010;33:1911]. Diabetes Care 2008;31 Suppl 1:S61–78. (Level III)

29. Boule NG, Haddad E, Kenny GP, Wells GA, Sigal RJ. Effects of exercise on glycemic control and body mass in type 2 diabetes mellitus: a meta-analysis of controlled clinical trials. JAMA 2001;286:1218–27. (Meta-analysis)

30. 2008 physical activity guidelines for Americans: be active, healthy, and happy! Washington, DC: U.S. Dept. of Health and Human Services; 2008. Available at: http://www.health.gov/paguidelines/pdf/paguide.pdf. Retrieved May 16, 2013. (Level III)

31. Effect of intensive therapy on the development and progression of diabetic nephropathy in the Diabetes Control and Complications Trial. The Diabetes Control and Complications (DCCT) Research Group. Kidney Int 1995;47:1703–20. (Level I)

32. Effect of intensive blood-glucose control with metformin on complications in overweight patients with type 2 diabetes (UKPDS 34). UK Prospective Diabetes Study (UKPDS) Group [published erratum appears in Lancet 1998;352:1558]. Lancet 1998;352:854–65. (Level I)

33. Turnbull FM, Abraira C, Anderson RJ, Byington RP, Chalmers JP, Duckworth WC, et al. Intensive glucose control and macrovascular outcomes in type 2 diabetes. Control Group [published erratum appears in Diabetologia 2009;52:2470]. Diabetologia 2009;52:2288–98. (Meta-analysis)

34. Skyler JS, Bergenstal R, Bonow RO, Buse J, Deedwania P, Gale EA, et al. Intensive glycemic control and the prevention of cardiovascular events: implications of the ACCORD, ADVANCE, and VA diabetes trials: a position statement of the American Diabetes Association and a scientific statement of the American College of Cardiology Foundation and the American Heart Association. American Diabetes Association, American College of Cardiology Foundation and American Heart Association [published erratum appears in Diabetes Care 2009;32:754]. Diabetes Care 2009;32:187–92. (Level III)

35. Nathan DM, Kuenen J, Borg R, Zheng H, Schoenfeld D, Heine RJ. Translating the A1C assay into estimated average glucose values. A1c-Derived Average Glucose Study Group [published erratum appears in Diabetes Care 2009; 32:207]. Diabetes Care 2008;31:1473–8. (Level II-3)

36. Ceriello A. Postprandial hyperglycemia and diabetes complications: is it time to treat? Diabetes 2005;54:1–7. (Level III)

37. Weissberg-Benchell J, Antisdel-Lomaglio J, Seshadri R. Insulin pump therapy: a meta-analysis. Diabetes Care 2003;26:1079–87. (Meta-analysis)

38. DeWitt DE, Hirsch IB. Outpatient insulin therapy in type 1 and type 2 diabetes mellitus: scientific review. JAMA 2003;289:2254–64. (Level III)

39. DeWitt DE, Dugdale DC. Using new insulin strategies in the outpatient treatment of diabetes: clinical applications. JAMA 2003;289:2265–9. (Level III)

40. Nathan DM, Buse JB, Davidson MB, Ferrannini E, Holman RR, Sherwin R, et al. Medical management of hyperglycemia in type 2 diabetes: a consensus algorithm for the initiation and adjustment of therapy: a consensus statement of the American Diabetes Association and the European Association for the Study of Diabetes. American Diabetes Association and European Association for Study of Diabetes. Diabetes Care 2009;32:193–203. (Level III)

41. Salpeter SR, Greyber E, Pasternak GA, Salpeter EE. Risk of fatal and nonfatal lactic acidosis with metformin use in type 2 diabetes mellitus. Cochrane Database of Systematic Reviews 2010, Issue 4. Art. No.: CD002967. DOI: 10.1002/14651858.CD002967.pub4. (Meta-analysis)

42. Nestler JE. Metformin for the treatment of the polycystic ovary syndrome. N Engl J Med 2008;358:47–54. (Level III)

43. Home PD, Pocock SJ, Beck-Nielsen H, Curtis PS, Gomis R, Hanefeld M, et al. Rosiglitazone evaluated for cardiovascular outcomes in oral agent combination therapy for type 2 diabetes (RECORD): a multicentre, randomized, open-label trial. RECORD Study Team. Lancet 2009;373:2125–35. (Level I)

44. Nissen SE, Wolski K. Effect of rosiglitazone on the risk of myocardial infarction and death from cardiovascular causes [published erratum appears in N Engl J Med 2007;357:100]. N Engl J Med 2007;356:2457–71. (Level I)

45. Weise WJ, Sivanandy MS, Block CA, Comi RJ. Exenatide-associated ischemic renal failure [letter]. Diabetes Care 2009;32:e22–3. (Level III)

46. Exenatide (marketed as Byetta): acute pancreatitis. Food and Drug Administration. FDA Drug Saf Newsl 2008;1:12–4. Available at: http://www.fda.gov/downloads/drugs/drugsafety/drugsafetynewsletter/ucm109169.pdf. Retrieved March 19, 2013. (Level III)

47. Precose (acarbose tablets) label. Wayne (NJ): Bayer HealthCare; 2008. Available at http://www.accessdata.fda.gov/drugsatfda_docs/label/2012/020482s025lbl.pdf. Retrieved March 19, 2013. (Level III)

48. Van de Laar FA, Lucassen PL, Akkermans RP, van de Lisdonk EH, Rutten GE, van Weel C. Alpha-glucosidase inhibitors for patients with type 2 diabetes: results from a Cochrane systematic review and meta-analysis. Diabetes Care 2005;28:154–63. (Meta-analysis)

49. Buchwald H, Estok R, Fahrbach K, Banel D, Jensen MD, Pories WJ, et al. Weight and type 2 diabetes after bariatric surgery: systematic review and meta-analysis. Am J Med 2009;122:248–56. (Meta-analysis)

50. Zimmet P, Alberti KG. Surgery or medical therapy for obese patients with type 2 diabetes [editorial]? N Engl J Med 2012;366:1635–6. (Level III)

51. Buse JB, Ginsberg HN, Bakris GL, Clark, NG, Costa F, Eckel R, et al. Primary prevention of cardiovascular diseases in people with diabetes mellitus: a scientific statement from the American Heart Association and the American Diabetes Association. Diabetes Care 2007;30:162–72. (Level III)

52. Fong DS, Aiello LP, Ferris FL 3rd, Klein R. Diabetic retinopathy. Diabetes Care 2004;27:2540–53. (Level III)

53. The effect of intensive treatment of diabetes on the development and pro-
    gression of long-term complications in insulin-dependent diabetes mellitus.
    The Diabetes Control and Complications Trial Research Group. N Engl J Med
    1993;329:977–86. (Level I)

54. Chew EY, Ambrosius WT, Davis MD, Danis RP, Gangaputra S, Greven CM,
    et al. Effects of medical therapies on retinopathy progression in type 2 dia-
    betes. ACCORD Study Group. ACCORD Eye Study Group [published errata
    appear in N Engl J Med 2011;364:190. N Engl J Med 2012;367:2458]. N Engl
    J Med 2010;363:233–44. (Level I)

55. Boulton AJ, Vinik AI, Arezzo JC, Bril V, Feldman EL, Freeman R, et al.
    Diabetic neuropathies: a statement by the American Diabetes Association.
    American Diabetes Association. Diabetes Care 2005;28:956–62. (Level III)

56. Edwards JL, Vincent AM, Cheng HT, Feldman EL. Diabetic neuropathy:
    mechanisms to management. Pharmacol Ther 2008;120:1–34. (Level III)

57. The effect of intensive diabetes therapy on the development and progres-
    sion of neuropathy. The Diabetes Control and Complications Trial Research
    Group. Ann Intern Med 1995;122:561–8. (Level I)

58. Xiang AH, Kawakubo M, Kjos SL, Buchanan TA. Long-acting injectable pro-
    gestin contraception and risk of type 2 diabetes in Latino women with prior
    gestational diabetes mellitus. Diabetes Care 2006;29:613–7. (Level II-2)

59. Palomba S, Orio F Jr, Nardo LG, Falbo A, Russo T, Corea D, et al. Metformin
    administration versus laparoscopic ovarian diathermy in clomiphene citrate-
    resistant women with polycystic ovary syndrome: a prospective parallel
    randomized double-blind placebo-controlled trial [published erratum appears
    in J Clin Endocrinol Metab 2005;90:3945]. J Clin Endocrinol Metabol 2004;
    89:4801–9. (Level I)

60. Palomba S Orio F Jr, Falbo A, Manguso F, Russo T, Cascella T, et al.
    Prospective parallel randomized, double-blind, double-dummy controlled
    clinical trial comparing clomiphene citrate and metformin as first-line treat-
    ment for ovulation induction in nonobese anovulatory women with polycys-
    tic ovary syndrome. J Clin Endocrinol Metab 2005;90:4068–74. (Level I)

61. Legro RS, Barnhart HX, Schlaff WD, Carr BR, Diamond MP, Carson SA, et al.
    Clomiphene, metformin or both for infertility in the polycystic ovary syn-
    drome. Cooperative Multicenter Reproductive Medicine Network. N Engl J
    Med 2007;356:551–66. (Level I)

62. Legro RS. Metformin during pregnancy in polycystic ovary syndrome: another
    vitamin bites the dust. J Clin Endocrinol Metab 2010;95:5199–202. (Level I)

63. Vanky E, Zahlsen K, Spigset O, Carlsen SM. Placental passage of metformin
    in women with polycystic ovary syndrome. Fertil Steril 2005;83:1575–8.
    (Level III)

64. Kitzmiller JL, Block JM, Brown FM, Catalano PM, Conway DL, Coustan DR,
    et al. Managing preexisting diabetes for pregnancy: summary of evidence
    and consensus recommendations for care. Diabetes Care 2008;31:1060–79.
    (Level III)

65. Ladner HE, Danielsen B, Gilbert WM. Acute myocardial infarction in pregnancy and the puerperium: a population-based study. Obstet Gynecol 2005;105:480–4. (Level II-3)

66. Kitzmiller JL, Buchanan TA, Kjos S, Combs CA, Ratner RE. Pre-conception care of diabetes, congenital malformations, and spontaneous abortions. Diabetes Care 1996;19:514–41. (Level III)

67. Freinkel N. Diabetic embryopathy and fuel-mediated organ teratogenesis: lessons from animal models. Horm Metab Res 1988;20:463–75. (Animal study)

68. Pregestational diabetes mellitus. ACOG Practice Bulletin No. 60. American College of Obstetricians and Gynecologists. Obstet Gynecol 2005;105:675–85. (Level III)

69. Hebert MF, Ma X, Naraharisetti SB, Krudys KM, Umans JG, Hankins GD, et al. Are we optimizing gestational diabetes treatment with glyburide? Them pharmacologic basis for better clinical practice. Obstetric-Fetal Pharmacology Research Unit Network. Clin Pharmacol Ther 2009;85:607–14. (Level II-2)

70. Cooper WO, Hernandez-Diaz S, Arbogast PG, Dudley JA, Dyer S, Gideon PS, et al. Major congenital malformations after first-trimester exposure to ACE inhibitors. N Engl J Med 2006; 354:2443–51. (Level II-3)

71. Albrecht SS, Kuklina EV, Bansil P, Jamieson DJ, Whiteman MK, Kourtis AP, et al. Diabetes trends among delivery hospitalizations in the U.S., 1994-2004. Diabetes Care 2010;33:768–73. (Level II-3)

72. Rasmussen KM, Yaktine AL, editors. Weight gain during pregnancy: reexamining the guidelines. Washington, D.C.: National Academies Press; 2009. Available at: http://www.iom.edu/Reports/2009/Weight-Gain-During-Pregnancy-Reexamining-the-Guidelines.aspx. Retrieved January 15, 2013. (Level III)

73. Weight gain during pregnancy. Committee Opinion No. 548. American College of Obstetricians and Gynecologists. Obstet Gynecol 2013;121:210–2. (Level III)

74. Kjos SL, Leung A, Henry OA, Victor MR, Paul RH, Medearis AL. Antepartum surveillance in diabetic pregnancies: predictors of fetal distress in labor. Am J Obstet Gynecol 1995;173:1532–9. (Level II-3)

75. Spong CY, Mercer BM, D'Alton M, Kilpatrick S, Blackwell S, Saade G. Timing of indicated late-preterm and early-term birth. Obstet Gynecol 2011;118:323–33. (Level III)

76. Rouse DJ, Owen J, Goldenberg RL, Cliver SP. The effectiveness and costs of elective cesarean delivery for fetal macrosomia diagnosed by ultrasound. JAMA 1996;276:1480–6. (Level III)

77. Use of hormonal contraception in women with coexisting medical conditions. ACOG Practice Bulletin No. 73. American College of Obstetricians and Gynecologists. Obstet Gynecol 2006;107:1453–72. (Level III)

78. Dabelea D, Snell-Bergeon JK, Hartsfield CL, Bischoff KJ, Hamman RF, McDuffie RS. Increasing prevalence of gestational diabetes mellitus (GDM) over time and by birth cohort: Kaiser Permanente of Colorado GDM

Screening Program. Kaiser Permanente of Colorado GDM Screening Program. Diabetes Care 2005;28:579–84. (Level II-3)

79. Rowan JA, Hague WM, Gao W, Battin MR, Moore MP. Metformin versus insulin for the treatment of gestational diabetes. MiG Trial Investigators [published erratum appears in N Engl J Med 2008;359:106]. N Engl J Med 2008;358:2003–15. (Level I)

80. Kjos SL, Schaefer-Graf U, Sardesi S, Peters RK, Buley A, Xiang AH, et al. A randomized controlled trial using glycemic plus fetal ultrasound parameters versus glycemic parameters to determine insulin therapy in gestational diabetes with fasting hyperglycemia. Diabetes Care 2001;24:1904–10. (Level I)

81. Gestational diabetes. ACOG Practice Bulletin No. 30. American College of Obstetricians and Gynecologists. Obstet Gynecol 2001;98:525–38. (Level III)

82. Hendrix NW, Morrison JC, McLaren RA, Magann EF, Chauhan SP. Clinical and sonographic estimates of birth weight among diabetic parturients. J Matern Fetal Investig 1998;8:17–20. (Level III)

83. Metzger BE, Gabbe SG, Persson B. Buchanan TA, Catalano PA, Damm P, et al. International Association of Diabetes and Pregnancy Study Groups recommendations on the diagnosis and classification of hyperglycemia in pregnancy. International Association of Diabetes and Pregnancy Study Groups Consensus Panel. Diabetes Care 2010;33:676–82. (Level III)

84. Screening and diagnosis of gestational diabetes mellitus. Committee Opinion No. 504. American College of Obstetricians and Gynecologists. Obstet Gynecol 2011;118:751–3. (Level III)

Studies were reviewed and evaluated for quality according to the method outlined by the U.S. Preventive Services Task Force:

I   Evidence obtained from at least one properly designed randomized controlled trial.

II-1 Evidence obtained from well-designed controlled trials without randomization.

II-2 Evidence obtained from well-designed cohort or case–control analytic studies, preferably from more than one center or research group.

II-3 Evidence obtained from multiple time series with or without the intervention. Dramatic results in uncontrolled experiments also could be regarded as this type of evidence.

III   Opinions of respected authorities, based on clinical experience, descriptive studies, or reports of expert committees.

Answers

14. D, 15. C
1. D, 2. C, 3. D, 4. C, 5. A, 6. A, 7. D, 8. A, 9. A, 10. B, 11. D, 12. C, 13. C,

Index

Note: Page numbers followed by italicized letters *t* and *b* indicate tables and boxes, respectively.

A

Acarbose, 32*t*, 39, 68
ACE. *See* Angiotensin-converting enzyme inhibitors
Acromegaly, 10
ADA. *See* American Diabetes Association
Adiponectin, 6
Alpha-glucosidase inhibitors, 32*t*, 39
Alpha-lipoic acid, 77
American Diabetes Association (ADA), 16, 23, 31
   "Nutrition Recommendations and Interventions for Diabetes," 23
   standards of care, 20–22
American Geriatric Society, 75
American Heart Association, 7
Amputations, 47
Amylin analogs, 32*t*, 39–40
Aneuploidy, 65
Angiotensin-converting enzyme (ACE) inhibitors, 42, 78–79
Antidepressants, 10
Antioxidants, 77

B

Beta-blockers, 10
Beta-cell function, 5, 6, 8
Biguanides, 32*t*
Birth control, 51, 68–70
BMI. *See* Body mass index
Body mass index (BMI), 12–13, 22, 24
Botanicals, 77
Breastfeeding, 14

C

CAM. *See* Complementary and alternative medicine

Cardiovascular disease (CV), 20, 36, 42
Case studies
   of a pregnant woman, 69–70
   of an older woman, 75–76
   of birth control, 51
   of gestational diabetes mellitus, 40–41
   of type 1 diabetes mellitus, 51
   of type 2 diabetes mellitus, 17, 40–41
Cesarean delivery, 67
Chromium picolinate, 76–77
Chronic pancreatitis, 9
Clinical trials
   Diabetes Control and Complications Trial, 18*t*, 19
   Diabetes Reduction Assessment With Ramipril and Rosiglitazone Medication (DREAM Trial), 16–17
Clozapine, 10
Coenzyme Q10, 77
Complementary and alternative medicine (CAM), 76–78
Corticosteroids, 10
Cortisol, 10
Counseling, 21*b*
   for management of diabetes mellitus, 20–22
   preconception care of a woman with diabetes mellitus, 55–57
   for the risk of congenital malformations in diabetic pregnancy, 70
Cushing syndrome, 10
CV. *See* Cardiovascular disease
Cyclosporine, 10
Cystic fibrosis, 3, 9

D

Deafness, 9
Depot medroxyprogesterone acetate (DMPA), 50

93

Sitagliptin, 38–39
SMFM. *See* Society for Maternal-Fetal
    Medicine
Society for Maternal-Fetal Medicine
    (SMFM), 66
Statins, 10
Stillbirth, 54
Sulfonylureas, 32*t*, 78
Surgery
    amputations, 47
    for obesity, 41–42
    Roux-en-Y gastric bypass, 41–42
Syndrome X, 7

T

Tacrolimus, 10
Thiazide diuretics, 10
Thiazolidinediones, 36
    contraindications, 75
    for treatment of diabetes mellitus, 32*t*
Tumor necrosis factor alpha, 5–6
Twin studies, 6
Type 1 diabetes mellitus
    case study, 51
    description of, 3

Type 1 diabetes mellitus *(continued)*
    insulin treatment for, 27–31
    mechanism of disease, 4–5
    prevalence in, 12
    prevention of, 14
Type 2 diabetes mellitus
    case study, 17
    description of, 3
    mechanism of disease, 5
    prevalence in, 12–14
    prevention of, 15–17
    risk factors for, 15*b*
    treatment for, 31–41

U

U.S. Department of Health and Human
    Services, 23
U.S. Food and Drug Administration
    (FDA), 17

V

Vanadium, 77

W

Wolfram syndrome, 5

Forthcoming Titles

Each monograph in *Clinical Updates in Women's Health Care* is an overview of a topic of importance to obstetrician–gynecologists in practice. Upcoming titles include the following:

- Allergies
- Thyroid Disorders
- Autoimmune Disorders
- Sexuality and Sexual Disorders
- Nutrition
- Adverse Drug Reactions

If not previously completed, earn CME credits for back issues of *Clinical Updates in Women's Health Care*. Listed are recent titles. For a complete list of titles, visit www.clinicalupdates.org.

- *Addiction and Substance Abuse* (Volume XI, Number 1, January 2012)
- *Asthma* (Volume XI, Number 2, April 2012)
- *Sleep Disorders* (Volume XI, Number 3, July 2012)
- *Upper Gastrointestinal Tract, Biliary, and Pancreatic Disorders* (Volume XI, Number 4, October 2012)
- *Anemia* (Volume XI, Number 5, November 2012)
- *Obesity* (Volume XII, Number 1, January 2013)
- *Exercise* (Volume XII, Number 2, April 2013)

You can sign up for a 1-year subscription to *Clinical Updates in Women's Health Care* at the rate of $59 for College members ($105 nonmembers). Individual copies also can be purchased for $25 ($35 nonmembers). You can subscribe by calling (800) 762-2264 or online at sales.acog.org. Online access is available to subscribers at www.clinicalupdates.org.

The Editorial Board welcomes comments and suggestions for topics. Please contact the Editorial Board in care of College Publications (publication@acog.org).

CLINICAL UPDATES
IN WOMEN'S HEALTH CARE
Diabetes Mellitus
Volume XII, Number 3, July 2013

Test Your Clinical Skills—and Earn CME Credits

ACCME Accreditation

The American College of Obstetricians and Gynecologists is accredited by the Accreditation Council for Continuing Medical Education (ACCME) to provide continuing medical education for physicians. ·

AMA PRA Category 1 Credit™

The American College of Obstetricians and Gynecologists designates this enduring activity for a maximum of 5 AMA PRA Category 1 Credit(s)™. Physicians should only claim credit commensurate with the extent of their participation in the activity.

College Cognate Credit

The American College of Obstetricians and Gynecologists designates this enduring activity for a maximum of 5 Category 1 College Cognate Credits. The College has a reciprocity agreement with the AMA that allows AMA PRA Category 1 Credit(s)™ to be equivalent to College Cognate Credits.

Credit for *Clinical Updates in Women's Health Care: Diabetes Mellitus*, Volume XII, Number 3, July 2013, is initially available through December 2016. During that year, the unit will be reevaluated. If the content remains current, credit is extended for an additional 3 years.

Actual time spent completing this activity (you may record up to 5 hours): _____.

To obtain credits, complete and return this answer sheet to the address shown below (only original answer sheets will be accepted for credit) or submit your answers online at www.clinicalupdates.org:

1. _____	6. _____	11. _____
2. _____	7. _____	12. _____
3. _____	8. _____	13. _____
4. _____	9. _____	14. _____
5. _____	10. _____	15. _____

ACOG ID Number _ _ _ _ _ _ _ _ _

Name _____

Address_____

City/State/Zip _____

The American College of Obstetricians and Gynecologists
Educational Development and Testing
409 12th Street, SW
PO Box 96920, Washington, DC 20090-6920

Reliable Take-Home Information for Your Patients

The American College of Obstetricians and Gynecologists' Patient Education Pamphlets are designed to complement and supplement the information and advice you provide in the office. After you talk to your patients about diabetes mellitus, ensure they have accurate information they can refer to and share with their families and friends when they are at home.

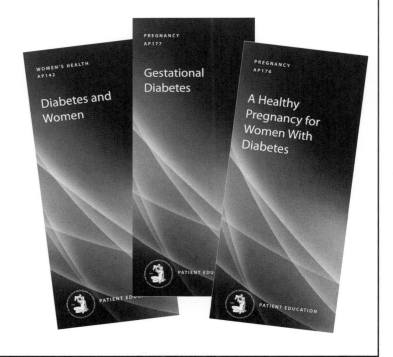